Pricing Policy in the Social Sectors

Cost Recovery for Education and Health in Developing Countries

Emmanuel Jimenez

Published for the World Bank
The Johns Hopkins University Press
Baltimore and London

© The International Bank for Reconstruction
and Development / The World Bank
1818 H Street, N.W., Washington, D.C. 20433, U.S.A.

All rights reserved
Manufactured in the United States of America

The Johns Hopkins University Press
Baltimore, Maryland 21211
First printing February 1987

The findings, interpretations, and conclusions
expressed in this study are the results of research
supported by the World Bank, but they are entirely
those of the author and should not be attributed
in any manner to the World Bank, to its affiliated
organizations, or to members of its Board of
Executive Directors or the countries they represent.

Library of Congress Cataloging-in-Publication Data

Jimenez, Emmanuel, 1952–
   Pricing policy in the social sectors.

   Bibliography: p.
   1. Social service—Developing countries—Finance.
2. Price policy—Developing countries. 3. Education—
Economic aspects—Developing countries. 4. Public
health—Economic aspects—Developing countries.
I. World Bank. II. Title.
HV525.J56   1987   338.4'33621'091724   86-27590
ISBN 0-8018-3501-1

Contents

Acknowledgments v

1. *Efficiency, Equity, and Cost Recovery: A Summing Up* 1

    Efficiency and Equity in Current Pricing Policy 1
    Pricing for Greater Cost Recovery 4

The Issues

2. *Current Pricing Policy* 11

    Prices and Cost Recovery 11
    Prices and the Allocation of Services 22
    Justifications for Current Pricing Policy 23

3. *The Financial Crisis and Underinvestment in the Social Sectors* 27

    Social Objectives and Fiscal Constraints 27
    Alleviating Underinvestment 35

4. *Inefficiencies in the Social Sectors* 39

    The Mix of Services 39
    The Mix of Inputs 43
    The Access to Services 49

5. *Inequities in the Provision of Services* 52

    The Distribution of Subsidies 52
    Reasons for Inequities 57

Changing Pricing Policy

6. *Basic Principles Revisited* 65

    Pricing Policy for Efficient Provision 65
    Pricing Policy for Efficient and Equitable Access 71
    Technical Note 74

7. *Changing Pricing Policy in Education*   77
   Behavioral Parameters   77
   Prices and Expansion   83
   Prices and Efficiency within Schools   92
   Prices and Equity   101
   Private Schools   102

8. *Changing Pricing Policy in Health*   106
   Behavioral Parameters   108
   Prices and Expansion   114
   Prices and Efficiency   118
   Prices and Equity   121

9. *Feasibility of Policy Change*   124

Appendixes

A. *A Review of Alternative Pricing Policies*   131
   General Pricing Rules   131
   Basic Needs   133
   Distorted Markets   134
   Pure Public Goods   136
   Economies of Scale   136

B. *Pricing Policies under Budgetary Restraints*   139
   Fixed Subsidy Allocations   139
   Fixed Prices   140

C. *The Algebra of User Fees*   142
   Impact of Changes in Subsidy Allocations on Fees   142
   Impact of a Fee Increase under a Fixed Subsidy Allocation with Excess Demand   146

D. *Tables*   147

References   155

Index   164

Acknowledgments

A PRELIMINARY DRAFT of this monograph was completed in 1984 while I was a consultant to the Resource Mobilization and Public Management Division in the Country Policy Department of the World Bank. The initial work was commissioned and supervised by Lyn Squire and Nancy Birdsall. I benefited significantly from their general direction, as well as from comments by other staff and consultants, including Martha Ainsworth, Trent Bertrand, and Oey A. Meesook. Punam Chuhan and Rama Seth provided research assistance. In mid-1984 the paper was presented at a conference sponsored by the Country Policy Department on "User Charges and Cost Recovery in the Social Sectors."

The manuscript was revised and updated in 1985 after I joined the Bank's Education and Training Department as an economist. The revision benefited substantially from parallel and collaborative policy work I did with George Psacharopoulos and Jee-Peng Tan on the financing of education. My discussions with them are reflected in many parts of the text, particularly in chapter 7. Any remaining omissions are my responsibility.

I would like to acknowledge the considerable editorial assistance of Barbara de Boinville and Richard Kollodge. Many typists labored professionally on the many drafts, including Teresa Hawkins, Setsuko Oiyama, Peggy Pender, and Althea Skeete.

1

Efficiency, Equity, and Cost Recovery: A Summing Up

PRICES HAVE GENERALLY PLAYED a minor role in generating resources for educational and health services in developing countries and have not been used to determine who should have access to them. Instead, the public sector, which is the most important provider of most of these services, has traditionally relied on general revenues for financing. These revenues, in turn, are financed through direct or indirect taxes, inflation, or budgetary deficits supported by domestic and foreign borrowing.

Tightened budgets have forced many developing countries to make painful choices regarding the financing and provision of their major social services. Competition for scarce government resources is becoming more intense. Unless they find alternative sources of funding, policymakers must either scale down their expectations regarding how much their economies can devote to these services or dilute quality. In either case, they run the risk of sacrificing long-term development to meet short-term exigencies.

This book reviews recent research—much of it supported by the World Bank—on the desirability of increasing the role of prices in financing and allocating educational and health services, usually the largest components of the social sector budget. The book describes current pricing policy and its effect on efficiency and equity. It then shows how efficiency and equity can be improved by adjusting cost-recovery policies.

Efficiency and Equity in Current Pricing Policy

Most prices for publicly provided educational and health services are very low or nonexistent. Even if prices are defined to include any charges levied on users of a service, the proportion of a government's cost that is recovered through pricing revenue remains small. Although data are scarce and some may not be strictly comparable, chapter 2 examines this problem and provides a rough indication of pricing trends.

In twenty-eight developing countries, the public cost recovered through prices for higher education is 9 percent; secondary education, 15 percent; and primary education, 5 percent. In health, the recovered cost is 7 percent. These figures must be revised upward somewhat if the percentage of social cost borne by users is calculated. A proportion of the cost may be borne directly by users and not reimbursed by public providers—such as the forgone income of years of schooling or the transport cost of traveling to a clinic. However, even if these figures are taken into account, the proportion of social cost recovered from users is relatively small.

Low or nonexistent prices tend to apply across the board for different types of services, as well as for different types of individuals. For example, in many countries free education from primary school to university is guaranteed for those who are able to obtain access, regardless of their income. The same can be said for many types of health services.

Traditional economic justifications for heavily subsidized educational and health services are numerous: benefits flow not only to individuals but also to society at large (externalities); small private providers operate inefficiently (scale economies); financial and labor markets are distorted; and the costs of collecting and processing fee revenue are high. These reasons, while valid for some social services, are not valid for all. Moreover, they do not justify the most popular pricing policy—free educational and health facilities for all users. Blanket policies have led to inefficiency and inequity.

Efficiency

Contrary to intentions, current pricing policies have made the provision of educational and health services less efficient. Signs of this inefficiency are underinvestment in these sectors relative to others, misallocation of resources within each sector, and an inability to ration services according to need.

Chapter 3 documents the financial crisis confronting the social sectors. For many governments, the real resources spent on educational and health services have been declining or rising at a rate slower than the population growth rate. Moreover, expenditures by both the public and private sectors of most developing countries are far less than the amounts needed to meet their stated social goals, such as universal primary education and access to primary health care. One estimate of the cost of financing a so-called basic human development package implies budget shortfalls for the average developing country as high as 17 percent of gross national product (GNP) (Meerman 1980).

These trends are disturbing because of the evidence that there is underinvestment in these sectors: high social rates of return are persistently found. Budgetary constraints have particularly affected recurrent expenditures overall, with drastic repercussions for health and education, where these expenditures represent the bulk of spending. At the same time, there is excess demand for many social services and an observed willingness to pay for them. Current fee policies are not flexible enough to use this demand to mobilize financial resources.

Current pricing policy has also contributed to inefficiency within the social services, as documented in chapter 4. This is partially reflected in a disproportionate allocation of resources for services with low social returns. Uniformly low prices for different types of services imply large subsidies for high-cost services without correspondingly high levels of benefits. For example, in the poorest countries in sub-Saharan Africa, public expenditures for education have been concentrated in higher education. At that level of schooling, students receive not only free tuition, but also living allowances that far exceed what is required. Allowances are nearly as high as starting wages in the working world. Under tight budgetary restraints, allocations for higher education come at the expense of other educational services. In these countries, primary school enrollment ratios remain low and so does the quality of education at that level.

Another manifestation of inefficiency in current pricing policy is the increased unit cost of providing any given educational or health service. A key to efficiency in provision is accountability. Administrators have to be given incentives to minimize costs. These incentives are less obvious in centralized systems where the few inspectors may be undertrained and inadequately directed or in systems where administrators are given lifetime job security. In general, inefficiency is exacerbated if there are fewer links among those who pay, those who provide, and those who use a service.

Finally, inefficiency occurs in the way subsidized services are allocated among the beneficiaries. To ensure efficient allocation in education, those who are most able to augment their productive capacity should be able to secure a place. In health services, at least those who have most to gain from being well or who are the sickest should be treated. Free provision of all public services, however, does not mean that everyone, and particularly those who would benefit the most, will enjoy this access.

When places are scarce, access must be rationed. Chapter 4 shows that this rationing has not been fully efficient in education. Because of privately incurred cost (mainly in the form of forgone income), free provision alone has not resulted in adequate representation of the brightest students from the lower-income groups. In many countries, these students do not even apply for entrance to institutions of higher education. Those who do are often at a disadvantage in competing for available places with students from higher-income families. Although they may be more able, they do not invest in tutoring or in extracurricular materials to assist them in passing entrance examinations. As a result, despite large subsidies lower-income groups are severely underrepresented at higher levels of education, where privately incurred costs are greatest. In some countries, higher education, and its attendant subsidies, is almost an exclusive preserve of the upper classes.

In the health sector, the most popular quantity-rationing device appears to be the queue. Although systematic evidence is not available, various field reports cited in chapter 4 are replete with examples of overcrowding in free health centers. It is only for inpatient care, where physicians have an opportunity to assess needs, that this rationing device may be efficient. For outpatient care, it is more difficult to ensure that those who need the service the most are given priority.

Equity

Another major justification for a policy of uniformly low prices is equity. To redistribute resources, social services should be financed from progressive taxes, rather than from price revenues. But this objective is rarely met.

As chapter 5 indicates, progressive redistribution has not always taken place. Uniformly low prices mean that the most costly services (for example, higher education or health care in urban hospitals) are subsidized the most heavily. For reasons mentioned in the above discussion on access, higher-income groups tend to consume more of these services. In the case of education, high personal costs make it prohibitive for lower-income groups to compete successfully with higher-income groups for the subsidized school places. In the case of health, many of the subsidized services are in urban areas inaccessible to the rural population.

The tendency toward inequity is not reversed even when the sources of financing are considered. Although most countries have progressive personal income taxes, these taxes account for a relatively small proportion of collections. The incidence of indirect and foreign trade taxes, which are the bulk of revenues, is not progressive, according to evidence cited in chapter 5.

Pricing for Greater Cost Recovery

Given the inefficiency and inequity of current pricing policy, what is an appropriate response? The rest of this book examines the role of increased prices in recovering a greater proportion of cost in education and health. Chapter 6 reviews basic pricing principles and the tools of applied welfare economics. Chapters 7 and 8 discuss the implications for the education and health sectors.

The general analytical framework in chapter 6 is standard partial equilibrium analysis. Although a general equilibrium approach is beyond the scope of this book, since it would require a relatively complex extension of the existing literature, general equilibrium interactions are discussed qualitatively wherever possible.

A move away from across-the-board zero pricing for all educational and health services is advocated. Pricing policies across all types of publicly provided services should not be uniform but should differ depending upon the "public goods" characteristics of the social service. If the externalities and scale economies are great or if exclusivity of use cannot be enforced, the role for subsidies in financing a public service is increased.

Pricing policies should also depend upon initial market conditions: how much of a service is being demanded relative to supply at current prices? For example, if public budgets have fixed subsidy allocations to a given service and if there is excess demand for that service, then prices could be raised. The revenue could be used to finance expansion of the service with the highest social return. If the source of fee revenue is the same service as its destination, prices could be raised until excess demand for that service is eliminated.

For services that require relatively large outlays, such as higher education or prolonged hospital stays, efficiency and equity in pricing policy depend upon the development of related markets. For example, education fees could be accompanied by credit schemes, and medical insurance schemes could be introduced.

Efficiency and equity are also improved by differentiating prices, not just by type of service, but also by type of individual. In this way subsidies could be targeted toward low-income groups rather than distributed indiscriminately. If the costs of implemeting such schemes are too high, prices could be differentiated by groups of individuals, such as rural as opposed to urban residents.

Education

The applicability of increased pricing in education is reviewed in chapter 7. The case for greater cost recovery through increased user charges is strongest at the level of higher education. Most of the benefits flow directly to the student, and there is also excess demand at the currently low level of prices. Increased prices are thus unlikely to cause any decline in overall enrollment for most countries.

The disposition of the revenues would depend upon country conditions. Any extra resources generated through user charges should be devoted to the activity with the highest social returns. In countries that are far from reaching universal primary enrollment, these resources could be used to expand primary education.

For example, if all living expenses for higher education in sub-Saharan Africa were to be covered through increased user charges, the primary education budget could expand, on average, by 18 percent. If operating costs were also recovered, the primary education budget could be increased by 41 percent (Mingat and Tan 1985a). Although full cost recovery in higher education is not necessarily recommended, these figures provide a rough idea of the magnitude of change that would be possible.

In countries that are already close to achieving universal primary education, such as those in East Asia or in Latin America, high social returns may be gained by expanding some disciplines in higher education or by improving the quality of most levels of education. If there are no scale economies, a 10 percent increase in fees at higher levels would allow a 1 percent expansion of enrollment at those levels. With just moderate scale economies, however, such an increase could accommodate an expansion of 2 percent.

If fees are raised at higher levels and used to expand primary levels, equity should improve, given the current distribution of subsidies. There would be a countereffect, however, if those who drop out at higher levels are from lower-income groups. This effect could be mitigated if higher fees were introduced along with selective subsidies and, eventually, educational credit.

Health

Chapter 8 reviews recent studies of health services where increased cost recovery through pricing would be appropriate. Although it is more difficult to categorize health services than educational services because of the many different types, one useful distinction is between curative and primary health care. Most patient-related curative services are not characterized by externalities.

Compared with education, there is less systematically collected information about the market characteristics of curative services. Anecdotal evidence suggests that many countries have excess demand for them. In these countries, a 10 percent increase in fee revenue from curative services could increase the amount of the health services by about 1 percent if all of the revenue were used to finance service expansion.

If there is no excess demand, the impact on utilization of a fee increase (to counteract a decline in subsidy allocations, for example) would depend on the elasticity of demand for health. For the average developing country, a rise in unit fees of about 7.2 percent would be required to counteract a 10 percent decline in subsidy allocations without creating excess demand. This would result in a drop in utilization of about 2.5 percent.

The efficiency and equity gains from user charges would be enhanced in a system where medical insurance was widely available. Otherwise, it would not be feasible to increase user charges for high-cost services to levels near cost recovery.

Feasibility

The last chapter of the book, chapter 9, assesses the feasibility of policy change. Information about the costs of administering cost-recovery schemes in educational and health services is relatively scarce. This would be a fruitful subject for further research. But the fact that many developing countries are already instituting policies to recover more of their costs suggests that they can be implemented.

The Issues

2

Current Pricing Policy

As CHAPTER 1 MADE CLEAR, prices have been little used to finance educational and health services in developing countries and to determine who gets access to them. Governments have traditionally been the predominant providers of these services, and they have relied on tax revenues to subsidize users. The percentage of provider-borne costs covered by prices is small. In fact, many governments have strictly regulated the types and amounts of fees that private providers can charge users. This chapter examines current pricing policies in education and health in developing countries and the impact of these policies on cost recovery and the allocation of services.

Prices and Cost Recovery

When the user of a service incurs significant consumption costs, the relationship between prices and cost recovery is complex. In this book, price is defined as any user payments, per unit of a service, to the provider of the service. Cost recovery per unit of a service provided by the government will then be the proportion of its unit cost that is covered by price (p).[1] Unit cost is the sum (per unit) of the recurrent cost (rc), the annualized capital cost (cc), and any direct transfers (t) to the users, such as educational scholarships or health allowances. The net unit cost for the government (or unit subsidy, s) is

$$(2\text{-}1) \qquad s = rc + cc + t - p.$$

In symbols, a cost-recovery ratio for the government (rg) is defined as

---

1. Hereafter, "charges," "fees," and "prices" are terms that are used interchangeably. All lower case symbols signify a magnitude per unit.

$$(2\text{-}2) \qquad rg = p / (rc + cc + t).$$

From the social point of view, however, this definition is not complete. Because of consumption costs, users may have to make payments that are independent of price. These might include opportunity costs (*oc*) of time while the service is being used and any direct private costs (*dpc*), such as transport in getting to the service, net of any transfers paid to the user (*t*). In symbols, unit private cost (*pc*) is

$$(2\text{-}3) \qquad pc = p + oc + dpc - t.$$

Thus, the unit social cost (*sc*) is the sum of government and private net unit costs:

$$(2\text{-}4) \qquad sc = s + pc = rc + cc + dpc + oc.$$

A cost-recovery ratio for society (*rs*) can be defined as the portion of unit social cost that is recovered from the user:

$$(2\text{-}5) \qquad rs = pc / sc.$$

In this book, measures of the governmental cost-recovery ratio (2-2) will be derived for selected countries. Because of the difficulty of obtaining the appropriate data, only a rough estimate of the societal cost-recovery ratio (2-5) will be presented. This estimate, however, is still valuable. Governmental cost-recovery policy is not limited to setting *p*. Cost recovery can also be affected by setting transfers and choosing how much of direct personal costs (such as books, in the case of education) are provided.

The preceding definitions of cost recovery do not measure actual collections. They indicate only the proportion of cost that is intended to be collected. Thus, even the relatively low cost-recovery ratios cited in this chapter are underestimated somewhat. The extent of the underestimate varies from country to country, according to various reports cited in Ainsworth (1984), and cannot be accurately determined.

Cost-recovery estimates are difficult to make in many countries because social services, such as health and education, are provided publicly and privately. Private-provider cost-recovery ratios are higher than governmental cost-recovery ratios, and they frequently approach unity. Thus, an overall picture of cost recovery in the presence of a significant number of private providers must take account of the private providers' higher cost-recovery ratios.

Table 2-1. **Public Provision of Education and Health in Selected Regions, 1975-80**

Region	Percentage of students public schools, 1975[a] Primary	Secondary	Public expenditure as percentage of total health expenditure, 1975-80[b]
Africa			62
East	57	55	
West	82	70	
Asia	87	71	30
Latin America and Caribbean	87	67	51
Europe, Middle East, and North Africa	94	92	57

a. Tan (1985b) and World Bank estimates.
b. de Ferranti (1985).

Cost Recovery in Public Provision

The public sector has been the most important provider of educational services in developing countries. The most accurate indicator of this is public school enrollment. In 1975, for example, 57 percent to 87 percent of all primary-level students in Latin America, Asia, and Africa were enrolled in public schools. Fifty-five percent to 71 percent were enrolled at the secondary level (see table 2-1). The proportions at the university level were also substantial according to World Bank data.

These figures have significant implications for government expenditures, since fees recover very little of the costs in providing education. Table 2-2 summarizes the available evidence on fees as a percentage of costs per user in the education sector (rg from equation 2-2). Fees in education consist primarily of tuition, books and supplies, registration and entrance fees, examination fees, boarding charges, and charges to parents and community associations for capital improvements. In the thirty-six developing countries for which data were available, 39 percent, 25 percent, and 30 percent charged no fees for public primary, secondary, and higher education, respectively. Of those that did charge fees, the amount as a percentage of publicly incurred unit costs was very low: 7.9 percent for primary education, 14.7 percent for secondary education, and 8.2 percent for higher education. In the nineteen African countries in the sample, fees tended to be lower for higher education than for education at other levels. Whereas 42 percent and 26 percent of Af-

Table 2-2. Cost Recovery in Education: User Fees as Percentage of Unit Cost in Selected Regions, 1980

Region	Number of countries	Percentage of countries with no fees			User fees as percentage of unit cost[a]		
		Primary	Secondary	Higher	Primary	Secondary	Higher
Africa	19	42	26	69[b]	13.4	19.1	8.3
Asia	8	38	13	13	2.4	16.0	12.0
Latin America	9	33	22	0[c]	2.4	2.4	5.9
All	36	39	25	30[d]	7.9	14.7	8.2

a. Calculated as an average of all countries with nonzero fees.
b. For thirteen countries.
c. For twelve countries.
d. For thirty-three countries.
Source: Adapted from appendix table D-1.

rican countries charged no fees at the primary and secondary levels, respectively, 69 percent charged no fees at the higher levels. Moreover, of those countries where fees were charged at higher levels, the proportion of unit costs recovered was lower than that recovered at primary and secondary levels.

In addition to the direct governmental expenses that are not recovered through user fees, public educational costs are boosted by direct payments to students for living and other expenses and by transfers to subsidized private schools. (See appendix table D-2 for a breakdown of government expenditures for selected countries.) Approximately 37 percent of public education budgets for higher education and 21 percent for secondary education in 1980 in Africa were reserved for scholarships and welfare payments (Unesco *1984 Statistical Yearbook*).

Even though user fees as a percentage of unit cost are low, as indicated in table 2-2, they play a key role in financing certain types of expenditure.[2] This is because of the way that educational subsidies are distributed to various schools. In countries where school fees are retained at the local administrative

---

2. In many countries listed in table 2-2, government expenditures appear to be directed toward financing one major item of educational expenditure—staff salaries. Other operating expenditures are financed out of fees. For example, in Lesotho, one-half of all fee revenue is estimated to be used for textbook expenditures, one-tenth for school feeding, and the rest for maintenance and other operating expenses (Lesotho, Government of 1983). In Swaziland, a study of a sample of government and subsidized schools indicated that the share of salaries in government expenditures is equivalent to the ratio of unit fees to unit costs (Swaziland, Government of 1981).

level or are earmarked and passed on to the provincial or national levels, much of the user-fee revenue is used to finance teaching materials (Ainsworth 1984). Country-specific data indicate that users finance a large portion of several forms of teaching materials. For example, in Lesotho, all textbook expenses at the primary level and 63 percent at the secondary level are financed by user fees (Lesotho 1983). Similar findings hold for Malawi (Thobani 1983) and many other countries. But no systematic studies have evaluated whether the level of these fees has been appropriate to finance the level of expenses.

Educational fee revenue is declining for many countries. Zimbabwe, Lesotho, Kenya, Indonesia, and Botswana have abolished primary-level fees during the past decade. In other countries, user fees have not changed to keep up with inflation (Ainsworth 1984).

A similar pattern emerges in health services, although the public sector share of total expenditures for health is smaller than it is for education. The figures vary from country to country for definitional reasons, but gross estimates of public expenditures as a percentage of total health expenditures are about 62 percent in Africa, 51 percent in Latin America and the Caribbean, and 30 percent in Asia (table 2-1). In general, the percentage of public health expenditures recovered by user fees is small. As table 2-3 shows, in fourteen of the seventeen countries for which data are available, the amount is 8 percent or less. For many countries, this amount has declined in the past decade (Ainsworth 1984).

Fee policies vary among service levels, which implies that fees may account for a small portion of the overall budget, but are more important for certain types of services. For example, in Malaysia only 5 percent of total government health costs are collected by user charges, while 8 percent of hospital in-patient services, which account for over half of all health expenditures, are recovered through user fees (Meerman 1979).

These unreimbursed expenditures, or those not recovered through user fees, imply that education and health subsidies (direct payments or fees below unit costs) account for a major share of the public budget. For example, developing countries (not including oil-exporting ones) allotted more than 10 percent of their public budgets to education in 1980. In Africa, that number rises to more than 16 percent (see table 2-4). The percentage share of health expenditures in the government budget was about 4 percent for Asia and the Middle East, and 5 percent for Africa.

Social Cost Recovery in Public Provision

To calculate social cost recovery, as in equation 2-5, estimates of direct private costs in using a service and of opportunity costs are required. These estimates are available for only a few countries and vary across and within

Table 2-3. Percentage of Recurrent Public Health Expenditures Recovered by User Fees in Selected Countries

Country	Year	Percentage recovered	Note
Botswana	1978	2.8	
Burundi	1982	4.0	Ministry of Public Health expenditures only.
Colombia	1980	28.4	Percentage of the amount budgeted, both recurrent and capital. Increased from 11.9 percent in 1975.
Ghana	1976–77	3.0	Percentage of recurrent expenditures. Declined from 4.9 percent in 1966–67.
Indonesia	1980–81	15.5	Expenditures at all levels of government. If standard payroll deductions for insurance are included, 17.1 percent.
Jordan	1982	13.2	
Lesotho	1980–81	6.0	Increased from 11 percent in 1970–71 to 16 percent in 1974–75. Since then, declined.
Malawi	1980–81	3.0	
Pakistan	1980–81	2.5	Expenditures at all levels of government.
Peru	1981	8.0	Percentage of both capital and recurrent expenditures.
Philippines	1981	6.8	Ministry of Health expenditures only. Declined from 14 percent in 1978.
Rwanda	1977	7.0	Total revenue, including payroll deductions, was 16.5 percent of expenditures.
Sri Lanka	1982	0.7	
Sudan	1980–81	1.4	Hospital and other fees, central government only (which accounts for only one-fourth of total expenditures on health).
Togo	1979	6.0	Excludes fees from and budget of Lomé University Hospital Center.
Tunisia	1982–83	2.0	
Zimbabwe	1980–81	2.2	Ministry of Health expenditures only. Excludes budget of Parirenyatwa Hospital. Declined from 9.5 percent in 1974–75.

Sources: Ainsworth (1984) and de Ferranti (1985).

Table 2-4. **Public Expenditures on Education and Health, as Percentage of State Budget in Selected Regions, 1980**

Region	Education[a]	Health[b]
Africa		
East	14.1	5.3
West	21.5	4.7
Asia		
East Asia and Pacific	14.0	5.1
South Asia	8.8	3.7
Latin America	16.4	8.2
Europe, Middle East, and North Africa	14.6	4.2
Developing countries	15.5	5.4

a. Unesco, *1984 Statistical Yearbook*, eighty-four countries.
b. de Ferranti (1985).

countries. Nevertheless, averages can be used to approximate overall social cost recovery.

In education, there are other expenses aside from direct monetary expenditures on tuition, books, and supplies. Expenditures for transport to school, uniforms, and school-provided meals, in excess of what would normally have been spent on transport, clothing, and food if the child had not gone to school, must be considered. There are also indirect expenses, such as the opportunity cost of having a child in school instead of at home working for the family business.

Information on the composition of personal education costs incurred by households in developing countries is limited by the paucity of studies. Nevertheless, it is clear from table 2-5 that fees represent only a small portion of total personal costs to the household. Opportunity costs, however, may be substantial at all education levels, especially in rural areas, and at secondary and higher levels in urban areas.

Actual earnings of school-age children were used to calculate the opportunity costs of schooling among the poorest 70 percent of urban households in El Salvador. Earnings of children out of school were compared with children of similar ages in school. The results, shown in table 2-6, indicate that the average household's educational opportunity cost, measured as the current expected income of those members in school, is about 4 percent of household income. The opportunity cost is, on average, 43 percent of total educational costs to the household. Opportunity costs are lower for lower-income households because the number of schoolchildren, particularly at higher levels of schooling, is lower.

Table 2-5. Private Costs of Publicly Provided Educational Services in Selected Countries
(current U.S. dollars)

Country	Survey year	Per capita income in survey year	Type of service	Average bursary provided	Fees	Indirect costs[a]	Opportunity costs
Kenya	1980	420	Rural primary	0	0	9	0
Malawi	1983	210	Standard 8	0	5	34	—
			Secondary	—	86	126	—
Malaysia	1974	680	Primary	1	2	51	—
			Secondary	5	30	123	—
			Postsecondary	7	141	236	—
Mali	1981	190	Rural primary	0	2	5	0
Tanzania	1981	280	Secondary	0	0	137	1,115[b]

— Not available.

a. Includes transport; auxiliary materials such as books, school supplies, and uniforms; and board and lodging if they are available. Some indirect costs are living costs that households might have had to incur had a member of the household not gone to school.

b. As perceived by the student.

Sources: Bertrand and Griffin (1983) for Kenya; Tan, Lee, and Mingat (1984) for Malawi; Meerman (1979) for Malaysia; Birdsall (1983a) for Mali; and Tan (1985a) for Tanzania. Per capita income from World Bank data.

Table 2-6. Opportunity Costs (OC) of Education by Income Quintile in El Salvador Urban Households
(1980 colones a month)

Household income quintile	Average household income	Average education expenditure	OC by education level[a] Primary	OC by education level[a] Secondary	OC by education level[a] Tertiary	OC for all education levels	Total cost (average OC plus average education expenditure)	Average education expenditure as percentage of household expenditure	OC as percentage of total cost
1	156.65	6.27	0.20	3.90	0.0	4.10	10.37	4.2	39.5
2	289.31	10.80	0.60	12.80	3.50	3.80	14.60	3.8	26.0
3	410.65	14.37	0.40	11.70	1.90	14.00	28.37	3.5	49.3
4	557.86	21.76	0.40	15.60	6.90	22.90	44.66	3.9	51.3
5	948.92	53.14	1.00	23.40	8.80	33.00	86.14	5.9	38.3
Total	477.74	19.59	0.60	11.70	2.50	14.80	34.39	4.3	43.0

Note: In 1980 US$1.00 = 2.5 colones.

a. Expected income of household members in school.

Source: Data tapes were obtained from the Evaluation Unit, Fundación Salvadoreña de Desarrollo y Vivienda Minima (FSDVM). The sample is from the city of Santa Ana.

To obtain an approximation of the social cost-recovery rate in education, it is useful first to rewrite expression 2-5 as

$$rs = \frac{p + oc + dpc - t}{rc + cc + dpc + oc}$$

$$rs = \frac{p}{rc + cc + t} \times \frac{\{1 + [(oc + dpc - t)/p]\}}{\{1 + [(oc + dpc - t)/(rc + cc + t)]\}}$$

(2-6) $$rs = rg \frac{1 + a_1}{1 + a_2},$$

where

$$a_1 = \frac{oc + dpc - t}{p} = \frac{\text{nonprice private costs}}{\text{price}}$$

$$a_2 = \frac{oc + dpc - t}{rc + cc + t} = \frac{\text{nonprice private costs}}{\text{government costs}}.$$

Thus, in general, social cost recovery in education depends on the ratio of nonprice private costs (opportunity costs and direct payments) to government costs and to prices. A reasonable assumption is that nonprice private costs are about one-half of government costs or $a_2 = 0.5$. The expression a_1 can then be calculated from appendix table D-1 for several countries in Asia, Africa, and Latin America to estimate equation 2-6, as shown in table 2-7.

In health care as in education, fee payments make up only a portion of total expenditures. These fees, which are for services and drugs, vary depending upon the mix of services consumed by the household. Other expenses to the user include transport to the health facility as well as the opportunity cost of lost earnings by those who are ill and by those who accompany them to the health facility. Because there is very little information on these other costs, it is impossible to make general conclusions about what percentage of health-related expenditures incurred by households is devoted to fees.

Table 2-7. Social Cost-Recovery Ratios in Education in Selected Regions

Region	Primary	Secondary	Higher
Africa	14.5	18.0	8.6
Asia	8.8	19.3	18.5
Latin America	11.6	13.6	18.8
All	12.4	18.2	15.6

Level of education spans Primary, Secondary, Higher.

Source: Calculated from appendix table D-1.

Opportunity costs are not as significant in the utilization of health services as for education. Thus, the social cost recovery ratios (rs) for publicly provided health services do not deviate markedly from government ratios (rg).

The Role of Private Providers in Cost Recovery

Overall cost recovery in social services also depends upon private providers, who rely more on prices to mobilize resources than their public counterparts do. But a significant proportion of privately provided education and health services in some developing countries is partially subsidized by the public sector.

For education, both intercountry and intracountry subsidization varies substantially. In Kenya in 1980 and 1981, 9 percent of the total public budget for secondary education went to assist private harambee (cooperative) schools, which accounted for 35 percent of total private school enrollment (Bertrand and Griffin 1983, 18–19). In Lesotho, churches own and operate 97 percent of the primary schools and 86 percent of the secondary schools, but the government trains, appoints, and pays teachers; administers examinations; reviews and authorizes curricula; opens and closes schools; and inspects the operation of all schools. A similar system operates in Mauritius.

This type of private-public venture is less prevalent in Asian and Latin American countries. In the Philippines, for example, donations and grants cover only about 1 percent of all revenues received by private schools. A survey of private education in five Latin American countries (Bolivia, Colombia, Mexico, Peru, and Venezuela) indicated that state subsidies are small and are given only to special schools (Muñoz and Hernandez 1978). By contrast Chile in 1983 transferred to private institutions about 20 percent of its public education budget for primary and secondary schools (Castañeda 1984).

In those countries where the private sector operates in health, private payments comprise a significant proportion—as high as 32 to 88 percent—of total health care costs (de Ferranti 1985, 9). The extent to which private sector providers recover the full amount of costs through user charges depends upon the country. The private sector is often partially subsidized, either by the government or by outside agencies, such as religious groups. Nevertheless, privately run health facilities tend to charge higher fees than do public providers for similar services. When this is taken into account, the share of private payments, including user fees and insurance premiums, for developing countries as a whole is 78 percent (de Ferranti 1985, 101).

The role of pricing in mobilizing resources for the private sector is also publicly controlled through regulation in some countries. In a few extreme cases, this has meant outright prohibition of private provision, particularly of education. For example, private schools and universities are prohibited by the constitutions of the People's Republic of the Congo, Ethiopia, and Nigeria (Cowen and McLean 1984).

A more widely practiced way of restricting educational services is through fees, student selection, curriculum development, and the hiring, payment, and qualifications of teachers. Although ostensibly less binding than outright prohibition, these norms may stifle private education. In Cameroon, for example, the government determines the fees charged by private schools. In Colombia and Chile, private school fees are also controlled by the government (Schiefelbein 1985; Castañeda 1984). Other countries, such as Jordan and Zambia, have simply declared that all primary education must be free.

These restrictions strongly influence cost recovery. Constraints on the operation of private schools mean that the system will have to rely more heavily on the subsidized public sector.

Prices and the Allocation of Services

In addition to mobilizing resources, prices can affect the allocation of educational and health services. As noted earlier, government providers charge low fees or none at all. Moreover, these fees are uniformly low across types of services, individuals, and groups. Because they are the same for everyone, fees generally do not play a large role in determining who obtains publicly provided educational and health services. The allocation of these services usually depends on privately incurred nonfee costs, such as transport to the particular service, or on rationing in cases of excess demand.

Most of the fees for educational services are uniform, and thus there is little attempt to use price to discriminate among users according to their socioeconomic characteristics. Ainsworth (1984) cites Indonesia as the only country in which prices are based on ability to pay. Malawi has a limited form of price discrimination: fees charged in rural and urban areas differ slightly (Thobani 1983). Fees are also uniform from one level of education to the next, except in Indonesia and Kenya, where fees rise with grades, and in Uganda, where fees for higher education are nonexistent. In most developing countries there is also no systematic documentation of large-scale disbursements for scholarships based on need. The negative impact of existing pricing policies on equity and efficiency is obvious.

While education fee policies tend to be homogeneous with respect to individual users, health policies vary—not only among categories of services, but also among categories of patients. Countries that provide free care to indigents include Botswana, the Philippines, Togo, and Zimbabwe. Some countries even distinguish among categories of illness, which reflects a certain amount of sensitivity to equity and efficiency. Botswana, for example, "charges lower outpatient consultation fees for chronic illnesses and treats communicable diseases free of charge" (Ainsworth 1984, 20).

Because the fees charged for most types of educational and health services to diverse users are uniformly low, they do not play a major role in allocation. One way in which allocation to services is currently determined is through other user prices that are not collected by the main providers of the service but are incurred as a user cost of consumption.

Where there is excess demand for educational and health services, rationing may determine allocation. Excess demand for higher education is especially evident in the low acceptance rates at many universities. Under these conditions, the most common method of allocating school places has been on the basis of students' achievements on entrance examinations or in school. In the health sector, the most popular quantity-rationing device appears to be the queue.

Justifications for Current Pricing Policy

The criterion for economic efficiency is precisely defined. An efficient, indeed optimal, allocation of resources among sectors means that all the economic agents are induced to produce and consume an amount that maximizes the total net benefit to society.[3] Marginal cost pricing produces this result when providers bear the costs internally (rather than imposing them on others) and users accumulate all the benefits (rather than conferring some on others). The unit price for a service should be exactly equal to the cost to society of the last unit produced. Does such a pricing scheme apply for the education and health sectors?

Efficiency

Educational and health services deviate from the marginal cost pricing rule for at least four reasons related to efficiency (see table 2-8). First, some of the benefits of these services may accrue not only to the individual user, but also to society at large. These extraindividual benefits are called externalities. Examples include the impact of literacy on lowering the cost of transactions among individuals in a society or the effect of an immunization scheme against infectious diseases. In deciding how much to consume, individuals

---

3. This amount implies that the additional benefit of another unit of consumption is exactly equal to the additional cost (see appendix A).

Table 2-8. Efficiency Reasons Why Marginal Cost Pricing May Not Work in the Health and Education Sectors

Reason	Efficient pricing scheme	Does efficiency pricing imply a subsidy?
(1) Positive consumption externalities	$p^* <$ MC: $p^* = 0$ only if the marginal social benefit is equal to the marginal social cost at a consumption level at which the marginal willingness to pay is exactly nil.	If MC $\leq$ AC (AC is falling or constant), an efficient pricing scheme implies a subsidy. If MC $>$ AC, the answer is ambiguous.
(2) Merit goods		
Lack of information	As in (1), if information programs are infeasible.	As in (1).
Lack of income	The optimal (first-best) policy is to have income transfers at $p^* =$ MC. As in (1), if income transfers are infeasible.	As in (1).
(3) Other public aspects		
Nonexclusivity	To circumvent free-rider problem, a benefit taxation scheme may be better than user charges.	If benefits flow to other than users, subsidy is needed.
Decreasing AC	$p^* =$ MC.	Full cost recovery from users is not warranted, unless a two-part pricing scheme is introduced.
(4) Market failures in other sectors	Depends upon distortion in the other market. In general, policy should attempt to correct for the distortionary effects of the related market. The first-best policy would be to correct the distortion (for example, by setting up an educational credit scheme).	Depends upon the nature and extent of distortion in related market.

Note: See appendix A for a rigorous explanation of the efficient pricing scheme for each case. MC = marginal cost to the provider; AC = average cost; p = price; p^* = efficient fee level.

generally weigh only the personal benefit against the personal cost; they should be induced to consider the impact of their consumption on others. A marginal cost pricing scheme that results in just enough consumption to equate personal benefit with cost is suboptimal.

Second, potential users may be unaware of all the personal benefits of educational and health services. In addition, even those who are aware of them may have insufficient income to consume the minimum amount considered socially desirable by public authorities, without unacceptable sacrifices in the consumption of other basic commodities, such as food, clothing, and shelter. Thus, educational and health services are said to have the characteristics of "merit goods." In other words, public authorities may have more information and resources concerning what is best for users than the users have themselves.

Third, some services are provided to the general public because access to them cannot be physically limited to those who are willing to pay. For example, insect spraying to control disease in a neighborhood benefits payers and nonpayers alike.

Fourth, marginal cost pricing may be inefficient because of distortions in related markets: markets for inputs (such as teachers, when their salaries are inefficiently subsidized); markets (such as the labor market) for other services for which the output (graduating students) of the social sector (education) would be considered as an input; and markets for financial services (such as credit for education and insurance for health). Access to credit and insurance markets, then, has important implications for efficiency. For example, without access to financing, a brilliant child from a deprived background cannot invest in higher education, even though the future returns may be very high. Thus, in the absence of a credit market, the social benefit of a unit of higher education may exceed the private benefit. For health, the relevant related market is insurance. Since many households cannot set aside a large amount of money to be used in the event of major illness, they may want to purchase medical insurance. But the lack of an insurance market prevents the efficient sharing of the risk of paying for major illnesses. Pricing subsidies are one way of circumventing these problems. If the lack of credit and insurance markets is viewed as a divergence between private and social benefits, the analysis for services with externalities would apply.

The labor market is also likely to be inefficient. The returns on investments in human capital depend upon the discounted value of future wage payments. If those wages are offered at a socially inefficient level, then marginal cost pricing in education would probably be inefficient. For example, if the main employer of university graduates (such as the civil service) offers a wage that is higher than the cost to society of attracting the labor from other productive work, more graduates would be tempted to go to school to secure those jobs than would be socially efficient.[4] (In technical terms, the marginal social benefit of a unit of education is less than the marginal private benefit.) These negative externalities imply that a price greater than marginal cost should be imposed. Negative externalities tend to offset the positive externalities discussed earlier and to reduce the need for price subsidies in education.

Equity

Much of public intervention in the health and education sectors has been justified on equity grounds. Some argue that public expenditures on social services can be used as a method of income redistribution, particularly if the services are financed by progressively collected revenues. Others claim that health and education should be considered "basic human needs," and therefore the public sector should guarantee access to some minimum threshold amount.

Challenging Traditional Justifications

The efficiency and equity arguments outlined above and summarized in table 2-8 imply a departure from marginal cost pricing. Appendix A presents the reasoning behind each recommended pricing scheme and gives specific examples. These arguments have traditionally been used to justify heavy public subsidization. The last column of table 2-8 presents the conditions under which efficient pricing schemes imply subsidization. As long as the average cost of providing a service is constant with respect to scale, marginal cost pricing is equivalent to cost-recovery pricing. Thus, prices less than marginal cost imply the provision of subsidies. If there are scale economies, even marginal cost pricing implies the provision of subsidies.

In recent years, however, many developing countries have been forced to tighten their budgets, and other conditions have changed substantially since their education- and health-financing policies were first established. Thus, it is time to investigate the record of public investments in meeting goals of equity and efficiency. There is wide room for improvement in both areas. The next three chapters reexamine traditional assumptions behind public intervention in education and health, and their findings lend support for greater private participation.

---

4. This might be so even if the limited number of government jobs resulted in unemployed graduates. If the decision to enter school were based on expected wages, there might still be an incentive to overinvest in schooling (Blomqvist 1982).

3

The Financial Crises and Underinvestment in the Social Sectors

BECAUSE OF LOW or nonexistent prices, publicly provided educational and health services have had to rely on the budgetary allocations of central governments. The fiscal crises recently experienced by many developing countries have slowed the flow of resources into the social sectors at a time when social objectives have been far from met. Even for those countries that have been able to expand their social services, the gap between available resources and social demands is expected to widen.

Social Objectives and Fiscal Constraints

Education

As table 3-1 shows, the social rates of return or the net returns that societies receive on their educational investments are high for all forms of education, especially primary education. The rates are generally computed by comparing the gain in earnings because of schooling with costs of providing that schooling.[1] The figures show, on average, that these rates are greater than the benchmark return on physical capital.

1. Many rate-of-return analyses in education require empirical refinements because of the unavailability of data. For example, estimates of social rates of return for alternative types of education represent only the monetary benefits of gains in earnings. They account for opportunity costs plus provider-incurred direct costs. Thus, the social rates of return to primary education are likely to be underestimated because private and social benefits are presumed to be equal, while the opportunity cost is probably overestimated. At all levels of analysis, tuition payments are ignored. In addition, several methodological problems arise from the use of aggregate data; from inattention to the effects of ability, employment, and the variance of income distribution; and from the underreporting of income. Nevertheless, these figures provide a generally accepted guide for investment priorities. For a complete discussion of social rates of return on education, see Psacharopoulos and Woodhall (1985).

Table 3-1. Social Rates of Return on Investments in Education by Country Group, Region, and Level of Education

Country group and region	Primary	Secondary	Higher
Developing			
Africa	28	17	13
Asia	27	15	13
Latin America	26	18	16
Europe and Middle East	13	10	8
Developed	—[a]	11	9

a. — Not available because of the lack of a control group of illiterates.
Source: Psacharopoulos (1985). Estimates based on sixty countries.

Rates of return have been documented in the urban sector, but the rural, agricultural sector also may benefit from social investments in education. For example, annual yields of farmers with four years of primary schooling are, on average, 9 percent higher than those of farmers with no education (Jamison and Lau 1982).

Education also generates indirect benefits. There is evidence of a complementary relationship between capital and education. Physical capital investments tend to be more profitable when workers have been educated and are therefore literate and numerate. In other words, educated workers operate production machinery more efficiently.

Education provides several other nonmonetary benefits. For example, educated people are more capable of complying with tax collection laws than uneducated people are because they have the skills to fill out tax forms. Increased tax compliance means more tax revenue. In addition, a literate population can learn about birth control methods more easily than an illiterate one can—an obvious benefit to countries interested in controlling population growth. Finally, literacy promotes citizenship: literate people can easily learn about laws and social mores (Haveman and Wolfe 1984).

Many developing nations, aware of the benefits from educational investments, have set constitutional goals to achieve universal primary education (usually obligatory school attendance for all children between the ages of six or seven and twelve or fourteen), eradicate illiteracy, or provide universal access to all levels of education. Developing and maintaining programs to meet these goals, however, are extremely expensive. Thus, the amounts that governments spend on education do not always meet constitutional obligations. Carnoy and others (1982) call the difference between actual educational expenditures and the amount needed to achieve constitutional or stated national goals the "legitimacy gap."

Table 3-2 presents the legitimacy gaps for primary and secondary education for six developing countries. These gaps are indicated in two ways: as the actual amount that countries fall short of their goals and as a percentage of the expenditure needed to meet the goals. For example, Brazil spent 33,300 million cruzeiros on education in 1978, but its goal would have required spending 44,000 million. The legitimacy gap, then, is 10,700 million, or 24 percent less than what Brazil should have spent in 1978 if it had met its goals for that year. A negative percentage means that a particular country's educational expenditures exceed the amount necessary to meet national goals.

Half of the countries in table 3-2 will have to increase their primary educational expenditures between 1978 and 1988 to meet national goals. Egypt's projected 1988 primary educational expenditures, for example, will be about 32 percent less than what is necessary to meet stated goals. The 1988 figure for Brazil (−78 percent) implies excess educational expenditure, but it is not necessarily correct because projected expenditures were based upon the country's unusually high growth rates during the early 1970s. Brazil's recent growth rate is much smaller than in previous years. From 1970 to 1975, the gross domestic product (GDP) grew at an average annual rate of more than 10 percent, but between 1976 and 1981, that rate fell to about 4 percent (World Bank 1983). Therefore, if Brazil continues to have a falling GDP growth rate, it might actually experience a legitimacy gap even though table 3-2 shows a surplus of primary educational expenditure in 1988.

In secondary education, large legitimacy gaps are apparent from the table in every country except Egypt, which plans on spending slightly more on education than is necessary to meet its national goals. All six countries will experience a legitimacy gap in at least one level of education in 1988.

Health

Although it is more difficult to estimate a summary measure of social returns from health services than from educational services, increased investments in the health sector are widely believed to contribute to economic development (World Bank 1980b, 30). For example, absenteeism related to illness can reduce the availability of labor. According to a careful study of tuberculosis control in the Republic of Korea, an optimal health program resulting in increased work life and decreased absenteeism would yield a return of $150 for each dollar spent (Feldstein, Piot, and Sunderesan 1973).

Table 3-2. **Legitimacy Gaps and Actual and Projected Spending in Primary and Secondary Education in Selected Countries, 1978 and 1988**
(millions of national currency)

Level of education and country	1978 Actual expenditure (1)	1978 Expenditure needed to meet goals (2)	1978 Legitimacy gap Amount[a] (3)	1978 Legitimacy gap Percent[b] (4)	1988 Projected expenditure (5)	1988 Expenditure needed to meet goals (6)	1988 Legitimacy gap Amount[c] (7)	1988 Legitimacy gap Percent[d] (8)
Primary								
Brazil	33,300	44,000	10,700	24	103,000	58,000	−45,000	−78
Egypt	74.2	131.9	57.7	44	120.3	162.8	42.5	26
India	4,450	7,700	3,250	42	6,500	9,500	3,000	32
Kenya	1,150	1,300	150	12	2,800	1,850	−950	−51
Mexico	25,600	25,900	300	1	46,500	36,500	−10,000	−27
Thailand	6,600	13,300	6,700	50	13,700	17,500	3,800	22
Secondary								
Brazil	12,400	47,900	35,500	74	37,800	63,200	25,400	40
Egypt	175	216	41	19	280	270	−10	−4
India	10,600	23,000	12,400	54	15,500	28,300	12,800	45
Kenya	315	1,180	865	73	770	1,680	910	54
Mexico	16,000	22,000	6,000	27	28,900	31,300	2,400	8
Thailand	2,300	6,500	4,200	65	4,700	8,600	3,900	45

Note: 1988 currency expressed in 1978 prices.

a. Column 2 minus column 1.
b. Column 3 divided by column 2, times 100.
c. Column 6 minus column 5.
d. Column 7 divided by column 6, times 100.

Source: Adapted from Carnoy and others (1982), table 1, p. 56.

An unhealthy workforce can result in low productivity. For example, a World Bank study showed that, in Indonesia, the prevalence of hookworm infestation in construction and rubber plantation workers was 85 percent, and 45 percent of the victims suffered from a resulting iron deficiency. Treatment of the anemic workers with elemental iron for sixty days, at a total cost of US$0.13 per laborer, increased productivity by approximately 19 percent. The resultant benefit-cost ratio is 280 to 1 (World Bank 1980b, 31).

Health is related not only to productivity but also to education because illness impairs students' ability to learn (Selowsky and Taylor 1973).

The World Health Organization's Alma-Ata declaration of 1978 outlines a "global strategy" for health for all by the year 2000 through primary health care systems (WHO 1981). WHO estimates that the annual per capita cost of implementing these systems would be an additional US$15 for most developing countries. Since per capita public spending is currently US$2.30, there is an average annual resource gap of US$50 billion for all the developing countries. Even if developing countries could fund as much as 50 percent of this amount, which would mean a quadrupling of average annual per capita domestic spending, they would have to seek external funding about seven times the present level of international transfers (WHO 1981). The growth of per capita domestic public spending, therefore, is not anywhere near the levels required to meet the goals of the global strategy.

The Cumulative Budgetary Impact

Even though governments and international organizations have decided that universal education and health care systems are desirable, they have not been able to cope with the financial problems associated with providing them.

Table 3-3 relates the combined government costs of basic human development packages to the resources that governments can collect. The financing of individual components "will normally range in costs from at least 11 percent to 21 percent of GNP" (Meerman 1980, 122). These figures imply that it is possible for low-income countries to provide comprehensive social service packages, but many will be unable to do so through government finance.

The recent worldwide recession has restricted the ability of many governments to mobilize resources to meet the health and educational needs of their growing populations. Per capita GDP growth rates from 1970 to 1980 have fallen in low-income countries (excluding China and India) by more than 50 percent from the previous decade (table 3-4), while population continues to grow. The gap between income and population growth is widening, which makes it more difficult for governments to meet society's health and educational goals.

Table 3-3. Hypothetical Government Costs to Provide Human Development Services in Low-Income Countries

Human development services and costs	Percentage of GNP
Adequate nourishment (to cover average food deficit in caloric requirements)	2–4
Universal primary education	3–5
Health care, hygiene, family planning (Malaysian standard)	1–2
Pure water and sanitation (universal water supply)	1–2
Subtotal	7–13
Associated investment	1–3
Adjustment for underfunding of recurrent costs	1–2
Subtotal	9–18
Incremental costs of covering the most expensive 85th to 95th percentile of the population	2–3
Total government costs	11–21
Total resources mobilized	10–20
Resources available for human development services	4–14
Shortfall (costs less resources available)	0–17[a]

a. Limiting cases of high resource generation and low resource requirements.
Source: Meerman (1980), pp. 124–29.

In addition, high administrative costs prevent many developing countries from reaching their "taxation potential"—the maximum proportion of national income that can be diverted for public services by means of taxation (Meier 1976, 271). Because inflation taxes do not need to be administered, they might be an easy alternative to mobilize resources for the public sectors, but there still may be severe adjustment costs as well as regressive incidence. Thus, many countries are left with the option of diverting increased resources to education and health at the expense of other sectors.

There is no evidence, however, that the average share of the public budget devoted to education and health has been increasing at an adequate pace. In fact, for many countries this share has been declining. Table 3-5, based upon data from the International Monetary Fund and other sources, indicates the extent to which the education and health share of the government pie has been shrinking for some developing countries. Although the share of education and health in total government expenditures has risen or remained stable

Table 3-4. Growth Rates of GDP per Capita by Country Group

Country group	Number of countries	Population (millions)	GDP per capita growth rates 1960–70	1970–80
Low-income	33	2,161	2.3	2.5
Excluding China and India		511	2.0	0.9
China and India		1,650	2.4	3.0
Middle-income	63	1,139	3.4	3.2
Net oil exporters		497	3.7	2.9
Net oil importers		642	3.4	3.3
Industrial market economies	19	714	4.2	2.4

Source: World Bank (1983), calculated from table 2, p. 150, and table 17, p. 180.

for the world, especially for industrialized countries, it has fallen, on average, for the non-oil-exporting developing countries since 1973. The downward trend in education, which was more pronounced between 1977 and 1980 because of the declining share of education in Latin American countries, is different from that in health, which seems to have been most affected between 1973 and 1975 by the adjustment to oil price shocks.

These trends differ somewhat across regions. The steadily declining share of health expenditures is most evident for Africa. Although the share of education expenditures in Africa rebounded some between 1977 and 1980, it has yet to reach 1973 levels. A recent African strategy paper by the World Bank attributes performance in both sectors to the "crisis management of recent years [that] has resulted in widespread neglect of programs dealing with the long-term constraints on development. In an environment of overall financial tightness, intersectoral competition for resources has made large social sectors the inevitable victims of budget cuts" (World Bank 1984b, 6).

These figures do not necessarily mean that the real public resources available for education and health have declined only during those periods when total public resources have declined. Frequently, educational and health expenditures suffer in relative terms, especially when total government spending increases or remains unchanged. For nineteen countries that experienced an average drop of 11 percent in real government expenditures, the average decrease in social sector spending was only 4 percent (Hicks and Kubisch

1984). Although this study used a broader definition of social sectors than just publicly provided education and health, data for those two sectors alone appear to corroborate its qualitative findings.

Table 3-6 lists the average growth rates of real per capita government expenditures for education and health. It shows no evidence that the social sectors have been more adversely affected than others when total government expenditures have been reduced. Between 1972 and 1975, when per capita total government expenditures fell an average of 30 percent for seven countries, average per capita health expenditures fell by approximately the same amount, and educational expenditures fell by only 3 percent. The same trend can be found between 1975 and 1979 for the twelve countries with declines in per capita total expenditures of 45 percent. Health declined proportionately, while education declined less than proportionately. These tentative findings indicate that although social sectors have been "squeezed" in favor of other government expenditures over the past decade, this has not occurred when governments have had to decrease total per capita spending. Rather, social sector spending has grown less rapidly during times of government expansion.

For example, more than half of the twenty-eight countries in table 3-6 experienced declines in per capita expenditures in education or health (or both) between 1972 and 1975, while eight experienced declines in total govern-

Table 3-5. **Expenditures on Education and Health as Percentage of Total Government Expenditures by Country Group and Region**

Country group and region	Education				Health			
	1973	1975	1977	1980	1973	1975	1977	1980
World	6.31	6.81	6.67	6.39	9.07	9.98	10.16	10.36[a]
Industrial	5.08	5.70	5.54	5.20[a]	9.94	11.28	11.47	11.73
Oil exporting	11.60	11.49	10.90	13.07[a]	5.20	4.20	4.07	4.72[a]
Non-oil developing	11.76	11.42	11.45	10.47	5.45	4.49	4.86	4.73[a]
Africa	18.62	15.71	15.68	16.76	6.12	5.35	5.46	5.09
Asia	9.31[b]	8.45	8.90	8.38	2.89[b]	3.26	3.27	2.82
Middle East	8.38[b]	7.41	8.17	8.72[a]	2.95[b]	2.96	3.33	2.73
Western Hemisphere	12.64	12.28	12.21	11.50[a]	6.03	5.41	6.15	6.10[a]

a. For 1979.
b. For 1974.
Source: International Monetary Fund (1981, 1982).

ment expenditures between 1972 and 1979. During the latter part of this period (1975–79), sixteen of the twenty-eight experienced real declines in per capita spending in education or health (a fourth experienced declines in both), while twelve experienced declines in total government expenditures.

These trends indicate that many countries are (and will continue to be) unable to allocate sufficient funds to meet their stated health and educational goals. According to the World Bank's 1984 *World Development Report,* the resource requirements to meet these goals are expected to increase rapidly because of unprecedented high population growth rates. To meet their goals in the face of troublesome financial constraints, governments often make unfortunate tradeoffs between quantity and quality that lead to a severe misallocation of very limited resources.

Alleviating Underinvestment

Because health and education in many developing countries are considered responsibilities of the state, users are often charged minimal fees or none at all. And since users' fees are limited, so is cost recovery. This means that the health and education sectors can turn only to the central government for help. But, as demonstrated earlier, governments' abilities (or willingness) to allocate more funds to these sectors is limited, even though demand continues to grow. The result has been underinvestment in both of these subsectors.

At the same time, the private sector has often been prohibited by law from operating in health and education, so it cannot compensate for inadequacies that arise in the purely public systems. Ironically, laws intended to shield society from the underprovision of a completely private market have prevented the sectors from responding to demand.

Simple tools of economic analysis illustrate the crucial role of pricing policy in alleviating underinvestment. Although this technical section can be skipped without losing the flow of the later analysis, it does show how economic analysis has been applied to pricing in the social sectors.

In figure 3-1, the private demand for a service is depicted as D_p and the social demand as D_s. These are not equivalent for reasons outlined in the previous chapter: externalities, failures in related markets, and concerns about equity. The total social marginal cost of providing the service is assumed to be constant at c. This unit cost is the sum of directly incurred private costs, c_p, exclusive of prices, and the unit costs borne by the government provider, cc_p.

The socially optimal amount of the social service that should be provided and consumed is that amount at which the additional gain to society from another unit of consumption is equal to the additional cost. In figure 3-1, this

Table 3-6. Average Growth Rates of Real Per Capita Government Expenditures for Education and Health by Income Group and Country

Income group and country	1972–75 Total	1972–75 Education	1972–75 Health	1975–79 Total	1975–79 Education	1975–79 Health	1972–79 Total	1972–79 Education	1972–79 Health
Lower income									
Malawi	1	−41	3	29	29	38	39	−24	33
Nepal	−2	4	22	24	48	42	39	108	52
Tanzania	54	11	60	−18	1	−83	66	24	—
Lower-middle income									
Bolivia	23	−27	−7	16	49	10	20	10	10
Costa Rica	−12	−20	5	50	83	736	32	46	778
El Salvador	14	27	−14	14	−6	22	31	20	4
Guatemala	2	−15	17	34	4	19	37	−12	10
Honduras	4	−1	31	43	20	−10	49	19	18
Kenya	0	1	1	34	0	21	35	10	23
Korea, Rep. of	−10	−10	−23	55	29	64	40	16	26
Morocco	86	45	4	17	38	−1	118	100	39
Paraguay	−3	7	−23	23	16	64	19	24	25

Peru	5	−6	−14	−86	91	−83	−85	−91	−86
Philippines	17	−13	50	−12	14	4	3	−1	56
Syria	99	−42	15	−25	2	32	49	−42	52
Thailand	0	1	−1	43	47	78	44	48	76
Tunisia	75	22	49	32	10	37	130	34	104
Turkey	8	36	−2	−36	−49	−39	−31	−30	−40
Zambia	39	2	9	−52	−49	−43	−33	−49	−38
Upper-middle income									
Argentina	−72	−67	−77	−99	−99	−98	−99	−10	—
Brazil	−5	−4	−4	−65	−72	−59	−65	−73	−61
Chile	—	1	−1	−1	−80	−85	−99	−99	−10
Iran, Islamic Rep. of	85	39	63	17	21	−12	17	68	42
Malaysia	32	28	33	54	13	10	54	44	47
Mexico	35	49	13	−6	−28	−36	−6	6	−27
Uruguay	−76	71	−42	−92	−74	−63	−92	−92	−80
Venezuela	26	18	−2	21	4	−9	21	23	−11
Yugoslavia	16	—	—	−44	16	−1	−44	—	−99

— Not available.

Source: International Monetary Fund (1982).

37

38   THE ISSUES

Figure 3-1. Pricing a Social Service

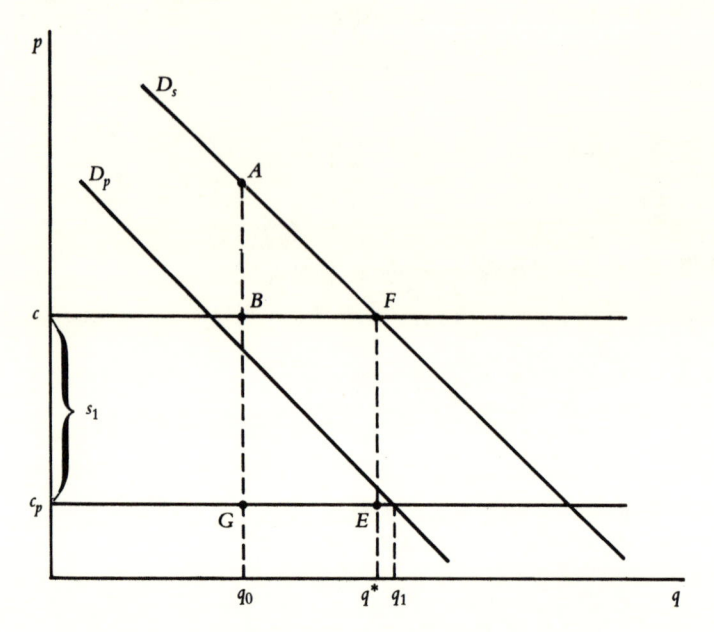

is q^*, which is the amount of the service where the marginal gain, measured by the social demand curve D_s, is equal to the social marginal cost, c. Although for some countries q^* may be equivalent to declared social objectives, such as universal primary education or universal access to primary health care, these objectives may imply magnitudes beyond q^*. They are frequently formulated without regard to c—the cost to society of providing them.

Suppose that prices are nil. (According to the previous chapter, this is true for many public providers in developing countries; almost all charge prices close to nil.) To ensure that the socially optimal amount of the service is provided, the public sector must offer a unit subsidy (s_1) equal to cc_p. At this level of subsidy, it must also restrict access to q^*, and there will be excess demand q^*q_1. The total subsidy allocation (S) required to finance optimal consumption would equal the area $cFEc_p$, which is $S_1 = (s_1)(q^*)$.

The problem arises because governments allocate subsidies of an amount S_0 less than S_1. Suppose this subsidy is equal to $cBGc_p$ less than $cFEc_p$. Given s_1, the total quantity that can be provided is q_0 less than q^*, and there will be social losses of an amount ABF.

4

Inefficiencies in the Social Sectors

CURRENT PRICING POLICIES have also contributed to inefficiency within each of the education and health sectors, as well as to underinvestment in relation to other sectors. In particular, prices are low, which implies that services are provided with heavy public subsidies. Moreover, prices are uniformly low regardless of the type of service or consumers' willingness to pay. As a result, governments have tended to allocate less to services with high rates of return, a lack of accountability has decreased internal efficiency, and spending has not been successfully targeted to those who could benefit most from the services.

The Mix of Services

Within the education and health sectors, various types of services are provided. Their different characteristics are important factors to consider in resource allocation. These characteristics depend upon whether the services exhibit externalities, whether users are knowledgeable about their benefits, and whether markets that affect them are distorted (see chapter 2). Using these criteria, analysts have grouped educational services into primary, secondary, and tertiary levels, and health into preventive and curative services.

According to the efficiency criterion for investing in social services, the most resources should flow to those services with the highest social rates of return. Although estimates of social rates of return are, at best, imprecise, especially for education and health, some quantitative and qualitative evidence suggests that the current pricing structure in many countries contributes to an inefficient mix of social services. Educational and health services with low social rates of return are generally more attractive to consumers and are provided more readily than are services with high rates of return.

Education

The pattern of subsidies leads to a great stimulation of demand for higher education. Households make judgments about sending children to school on the basis of the private rate of return, which differs from the social rate of return because of externalities on the benefit side or because of subsidies on the cost side. If households faced the true social costs of obtaining more education, they would confront a lower rate of return; instead, they are induced to obtain more schooling.

Table 4-1 reveals that for Africa the difference between private and social rates of return is greater for higher education relative to primary education. Much of this difference reflects direct payments to students for living allowances, which amount to 35 percent (East Africa) and 67 percent (West Africa) of the recurrent budget for higher education (World Bank 1986).

Yet, the social rates of return on investment in education decline as the level of education for all country groups increases (table 3-1). According to those rates, it would be most efficient to give priority to investments in primary education, particularly in countries in sub-Saharan Africa.

For any level of education, the social rates of return reported in table 3-1 were based on the difference between average earnings of graduates at that level and earnings at the previous level. These earnings were not adjusted for the possible effects of externalities or distortions in related markets, which may differ by schooling level. If these factors influence earnings, differences between social and private rates may be justified on the basis of economic efficiency. But even if externalities and labor market distortions are considered, the larger difference between private and social rates cannot be fully

Table 4-1. Ratio of Private to Social Rates of Return in Education

Region and country group	Primary	Secondary	Higher
Africa	1.42	1.34	1.77
Asia	1.57	1.10	1.33
Latin America	1.28	1.15	1.17
Average developing country	1.32	1.19	1.73
Intermediate[a]	1.38	1.15	1.55
Advanced	—[b]	1.55	1.32

Level of education

a. Cyprus, Greece, the Islamic Republic of Iran, Israel, Spain, Turkey, and Yugoslavia.
b. — Not available because of the lack of a control group with no education.
Source: Psacharopoulos (1985), tables 1 and 2.

explained. Positive externalities, such as good citizenship and the benefits to social transactions from a literate population, are apparent at primary levels of education but would likely diminish at higher levels. In contrast, the benefits of a greater amount of higher education are realized primarily by the individuals who consume the education and who are paid according to the value of their additional contribution to production. Therefore, externality arguments for subsidization of higher education are weak.

In many countries, reallocation of resources from higher education to expand primary and basic education would lead to gains in efficiency. In fact, estimates indicate that if public resources were reallocated to equalize the social rates of return at all educational levels, the efficiency gains would amount to 2.6 percent of GDP in certain African countries and more than 3 percent in some Latin American countries (Dougherty and Psacharopoulos 1977). These gains are comparable to a doubling of the public budget for education. Although this analysis does not advocate an immediate and drastic reduction in resources allocated to secondary and higher education, it does show that the present pattern of subsidies favoring secondary and higher education at the expense of primary and basic education is inefficient. In other words, current subsidies are not distributed in relation to expected social returns. There is a need, therefore, to increase the relative proportion of public resources devoted to primary education over other levels of education.

Health

In the health sector, it is important to distinguish between curative and preventive services. Curative health care involves the treatment of the sick. Preventive health care might include all services that ensure good health, such as immunizations and nutritional advice.

Some preventive health services have attributes that inhibit the role of prices in promoting efficiency: high levels of consumption externalities (immunization and disease control programs), unidentifiable individual beneficiaries, and a lack of information among users regarding benefits. As de Ferranti (1985) points out, it is probably impossible to implement national user fees for many types of preventive health services. For example, when a government agency sprays an area to combat insect infestation, it is impossible to identify who benefits and who is to pay for this service.

User fees may be appropriate for certain kinds of preventive and curative health care, such as in- and outpatient treatments, drug sales, and water supply; in these cases positive externalities are negligible since most benefits accrue to the individual. This is especially true for curative treatment of noninfectious illnesses. Society as a whole obtains no additional benefits from the curative treatment of ailments such as stomach disorders. And when patients return to work after this type of illness, there would be no additional social benefits if they were paid the competitive wage—the value of their marginal product (de Ferranti 1982; Blomqvist 1979).

Yet many countries charge uniformly low unit prices or give uniformly high subsidies regardless of the type of service. The greatest proportion of government health expenditures in developing countries goes for curative care, probably owing "in part to the professional bias of physicians and the mystique and popular appeal of hospital-based health care" (World Bank 1980b, 40). In Senegal and Brazil, for example, 72 percent and 85 percent of the health budgets of the central governments are devoted to curative care (de Ferranti 1983, 68–69). These figures indicate that governments may be investing the majority of their health care resources in services that promise only negligible positive externalities. This does not automatically mean, however, that all curative care should be abandoned or charged at full cost.

A comprehensive curative health care system can be very expensive for both consumers and providers. Consumers must incur private costs, such as transportation and opportunity costs, even when curative health facilities charge no fees. Also, curative services, such as hospitals, require huge initial investments, even though they are likely to experience decreasing costs—their average costs would decline as the quantity of services provided increased. Thus, within curative health care there appears to be little effort to differentiate prices according to the private costs of services and the individuals who must incur them. In particular, the rates charged for services in rural and urban areas tend to be uniform.

A Graphic Presentation

The differential welfare effect of a uniform pricing scheme on any two types of services can be illustrated with standard economic techniques. For this example, assume that prices are nil for all types of service. As before, D_p and D_s depict the respective private and social demand curves; c and c_p are constant total marginal costs and private costs, respectively.

In figure 4-1, zero prices result in an inefficiently low use of the service, since the presence of private costs inhibits demand too much. Thus, q_0 is less than q^*. One can argue that this figure depicts the case for primary education or primary health care, particularly in rural areas. Transport and, in the case of primary education, opportunity costs would be the principal components of private costs. The shaded area represents the social loss.

Figure 4-1. Underutilization of a Free Social Service

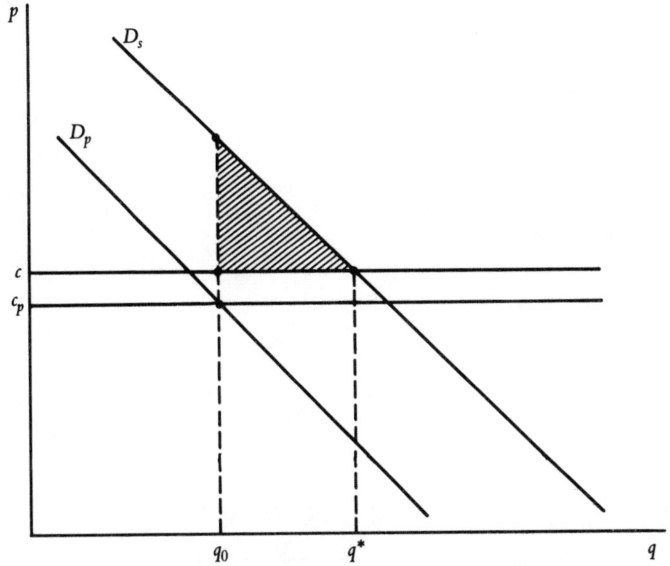

In figure 4-2, zero prices result in overutilization of the service but for different reasons. Some services, such as secondary education, may have substantial externalities, but private costs are a small proportion of total costs because of scholarships. In figure 4-2A, this results in overutilization of q_1 greater than q^*. Other services, such as curative outpatient care or university education, may imply high private costs but with little externalities. In figure 4-2B, this results in overutilization of q_2 greater than q^*. In both cases, the shaded area depicts the service losses if the service is not rationed.

The Mix of Inputs

A high level of unit subsidy has contributed to inefficiencies in the ways that various educational and health services are provided. Reliance on subsidies from central governments has led to inappropriate input mixes. In particular, this method of financing has caused underutilization of variable factors of production, such as nonlabor inputs, relative to other factors. There is a growing body of evidence that recurrent expenditures are being crowded out, even in cases where total health or educational expenditures are not being eroded. In addition, resources tend to be misallocated among variable factors, with labor inputs being favored over material inputs.

Figure 4-2. Overutilization of a Free Social Service

A. Low Private Costs

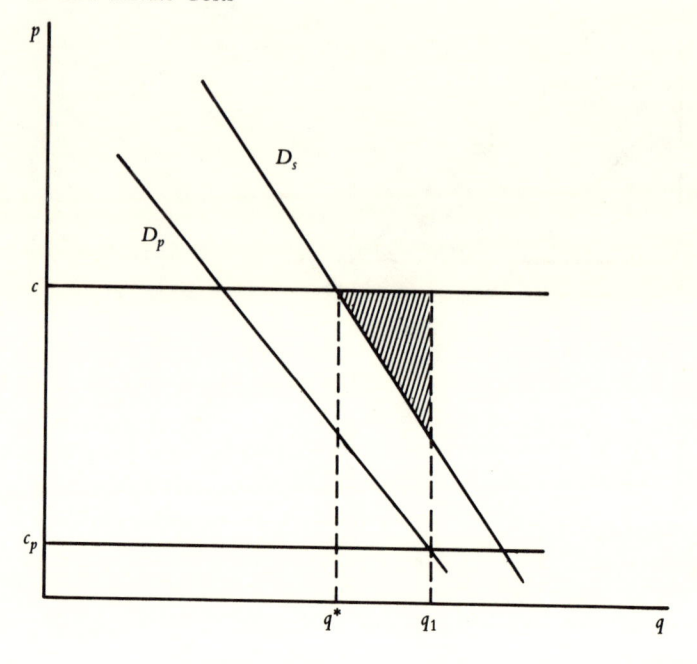

B. Low Level of Externalities

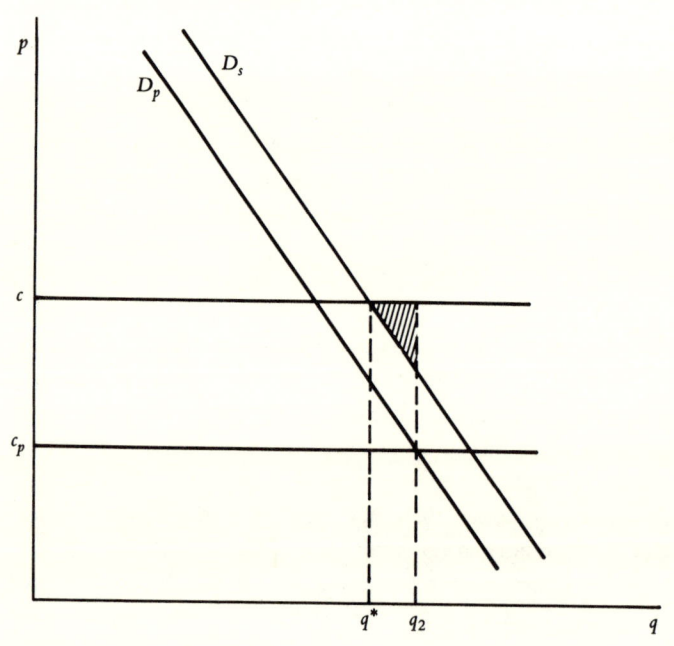

Frequently, the root of the problem is a centralized and rigid system of allocating expenditures. When the bulk of the funding comes from subsidies, field administrators are not accountable to the families who use the services they dispense. Rather, they are accountable to the funding source, which relies necessarily on preset formulas to allocate inputs. Then formulas often are inflexible to meet local needs.

Recurrent Costs

It is difficult for the analyst to determine a priori whether the mix of capital and recurrent spending is optimal. Depending upon technology and prices, it may be efficient not to operate and maintain existing capital stock at capacity. Recent studies of the so-called recurrent cost problem suggest, however, that at present there is a misallocation.

A program should not be established unless the resources that are required to set it up and run it year after year are considered to have higher returns in that program than elsewhere in the economy. If governments are incapable of drawing, to the extent that it is economically worthwhile, all the resources they require to run and maintain the program, a recurrent cost problem exists (Heller 1979; USAID 1982). There are many reasons why developing countries experience considerable difficulty in mobilizing the resources they need to finance sound economic projects. Table 4-2 summarizes the chief causes that are considered most relevant for certain countries. Most of the reasons are related to underfunding. Heller (1979, 40) notes that "the problem partly derives from the administrative structure common to the financial and sectoral ministries of developing countries which separates the investment and current budgeting functions." This problem is inherent in centrally controlled systems. It is difficult to plan, invest in, and administer programs in large systems when all financing comes from a common pot. Unforeseen budgetary crises create short-term expediencies that can be addressed by reducing the size of the pot.

The relatively high recurrent cost content in the social sectors makes them more vulnerable to budgetary restrictions than other sectors are. The amount of recurrent costs that need to be incurred to operate a unit of capital expenditure is higher for health and education than for other publicly provided services. Table 4-3 provides a comparison of the ratios of recurrent to capital costs.

Some recent aggregate studies of recurrent expenditures corroborate these conclusions. Between 1965 and 1973, although there was no serial decline in the overall share of current government expenditure in total government expenditure on average for a group of developing countries, "the strongest

Table 4-2. Causes of Recurrent Cost Problems in Specific Countries

Causes	Countries
Inadequate revenues	
Inadequate resource mobilization	Haiti, Malawi, Pakistan, Zaire
Sudden change in economic situation of country	Liberia, Mexico, Niger, Peru, Rwanda, Tanzania
Foreign exchange shortages	Burma, Liberia, Panama
Effects of poorly set producer prices	Mauritania, Sahel region
Project-specific problems	
Longer than expected gestation; poorly specified project technologies	Sahel region
Excessive investment activities in past	
Domestically induced	Guyana, Honduras, Madagascar, Malawi, Philippines, Sri Lanka, Tanzania, Thailand, Zaire
Externally induced	Haiti, Madagascar, People's Republic of the Congo, Philippines, Rwanda, Sahel region, Sri Lanka, Thailand, Togo, Zaire
Excessive growth of other nondevelopment expenditure	Madagascar, Mauritania, Niger, Pakistan, Tanzania, Zambia
Pressure to generate budgetary savings for investment	Honduras, Sri Lanka, Thailand
Budgeting difficulties	
Weak budget planning and forecasting; poor coordination of finance and planning ministries; lack of information; dichotomy of recurrent and development budget; management difficulties associated with multiple externally financed projects	Côte d'Ivoire, Honduras, Madagascar, Malawi, Nepal, Pakistan, People's Republic of the Congo, Philippines, Rwanda, Sri Lanka, Tanzania, Togo, Zaire
Earmarking	Costa Rica, Haiti

Note: The fact a cause was not listed by no means denies its relevance to a particular country.
Source: Heller and Aghevli (1985). Reprinted with permission.

evidence of a secular decline was found in the health sector" (Lim 1983a, 378). A regression of the share of recurrent health expenditure of total health expenditure with respect to time yielded a negative and significant coefficient (at 5 percent) for 40 percent of the countries. More than 60 percent of

Table 4-3. Recurrent Expenditures as a Proportion of Investment

Sector	Ratio of recurrent to capital costs
Agriculture	
Fisheries	0.08
Forestry	0.04
General agriculture	0.10
Livestock	0.14
Rural development	0.08–0.43
Veterinary services	0.07
Buildings	0.01
Education[a]	
Agricultural colleges	0.17
Polytechnic schools	0.17
Primary schools	0.06–7.00
Secondary schools	0.08–7.20
Universities	0.02–0.22
Health	
District hospitals	0.11–0.30
General hospitals	0.18
Medical auxiliary training school	0.14
Nurses college	0.20
Nutrition rehabilitation unit	0.34
Rural health centers	0.27–0.71
Urban health centers	0.17
Roads	
Feeder	0.06–0.14
Paved	0.03–0.07
Social and rural development	0.04
Tourism	0.05

a. The relatively high figures for education may be due to an underestimate of capital costs, some of which are borne privately, particularly in several African countries. This underestimate is not expected to be severe.

Source: Heller (1979), p. 39.

Latin American countries exhibited this result. Moreover, recurrent expenditure is more unstable than capital expenditure in the health and education sectors, the reverse of the trend in "hard" sectors, such as agriculture, transport, and communications. In another study, Lim (1983b, 450) speculates that "this might have reflected the unfortunate widespread tendency to treat recurrent spending as consumption and development spending as investment." These findings could be expected to be worse in the post-1973 period as a result of generally tighter budgetary restraints.

Observable declines in the quality of educational and health services reflect this pressure on the recurrent budgets. The operational effects of the problem have been bad maintenance and underutilization of the capital stock. This is often manifested in undertrained staff, or none at all. A case in point is Kenya's primary education system. In 1974, school fees were abolished for the first four years of primary education, and, in 1979, all other primary school fees were abolished. Enrollment in 1974 was 253 percent more than in 1973; enrollment in 1979 was 163 percent more than in 1978. Since the government could not mobilize the necessary resources to replace this financing quickly enough, the effects on quality were immediate. In 1974, the percentage of untrained teachers increased from 22 to 33 percent. In 1979, student-teacher ratios were allowed to increase (table 4-4). Given resource constraints, this reflects the tradeoff between increased coverage and lower quality.

In both sectors, however, the problem is most severe in underspending for nonlabor inputs, such as school materials, maintenance, and pharmaceuticals. This points to another difficulty: when a recurrent cost problem exists, the nonlabor component usually suffers the most.

Table 4-4. Primary Education in Kenya

Year	Gross enrollment ratio[a]	Percentage growth of teachers	Percentage of untrained teachers	Student-teacher ratio
1972	0.66	—	22	—
1973	0.69	6	22	32
1974	1.03	39	33	35
1975	1.02	10	36	33
1976	0.99	3	37	32
1977	0.99	1	34	33
1978	0.96	3	31	33
1979	1.14	1	26	40

— Not available.
a. Enrollment in primary schools divided by population of primary school age.
Source: Bertrand and Griffin (1983).

The Choice of Recurrent Inputs

There are several reasons why, in the face of tightening constraints, the pressure to forgo nonlabor recurrent expenditures is the greatest. One has to do with the strong labor unions; teachers in particular are a powerful political force to be reckoned with in many countries. Another simply concerns the way central authorities distribute subsidies. In many instances, staff are appointed from central ministries and are given field positions. Field supervisors, when told to cut back, have no leeway to do so through staff lay-offs; they must cut back nonwage expenditures.

For example, a recent study concluded that the increasing fiscal pressures on education over the past decade have affected the way the twenty-eight developing countries in the study "resolved the conflict between the budgetary pressures confronting all elements of the public sector and the political pressures for expanding enrollments and the attendant fiscal implications of such expansion" (Heller and Cheasty 1984, 23). The public sector response was to increase enrollments by squeezing recurrent expenditure per student, particularly at the higher levels of education. This was done primarily by allowing a clear deterioration in the share and level of real expenditure per student on nonwage recurrent inputs (table 4-5). In many countries, teachers' wages were allowed to increase more rapidly than were expenditures per student. This serious deficiency is reflected in a lack of books and other school materials.

The Access to Services

When resources are scarce, it is efficient to give priority to users who will benefit the most from a service. Because of externalities or failures in related markets, it is generally not efficient to rely solely on willingness to pay in determining this priority. But charging nothing or close to nothing also will not lead to efficient allocations.

In education, it would be efficient to provide priority access to those who are most able to augment their productive capacity. If there is some complementary relationship between schooling and innate ability to improve productivity, the most able should be ensured access. Because the distribution of innate ability is not likely to be correlated with willingness to pay, an allocation system that relied on the income criterion alone to distribute a small number of school places would result in an underrepresentation of the most able students.

Zero pricing schemes, on the surface, would seem to be efficient in this respect. Upon closer inspection, however, they also base allocations on

Table 4-5. Potential Indicators of Quality Change in Education by Level of Education, 1965–78
(percentage of countries)

Level of education	Wage rates increased more rapidly than expenditure per student — Latin America	Wage rates increased more rapidly than expenditure per student — Other middle-income countries	Nonwage expenditure per student decreased — Latin America	Nonwage expenditure per student decreased — Other middle-income countries
Primary education				
1965–70	53 (67)[a]	33	n.a.	n.a.
1970–75	27 (55)[a]	n.a.	n.a.	n.a.
1975–78	29 (71)[a]	20	n.a.	n.a.
1970–78	27	25	n.a.	n.a.
Secondary education				
1965–70	43	40	17	40
1970–75	70	71	55	71
1975–78	60	20	80	20
1970–78	78	25	83	25
Tertiary education				
1965–70	69	40	50	50
1970–75	50	50	50	50
1975–78	60	50	75	66
1970–78	80	100	100	100

Note: The percentages refer to the number of "unfavorable" observations divided by the number of total available observations in each category; thus, where observations are few, the description of the state of education may not be accurate.

n.a. Assumed not to be applicable for primary education.

a. Figures in parentheses refer to cases in which wages increased at least at the pace of expenditures.

Source: Heller and Cheasty (1984). Reprinted with permission.

willingness to pay. First, even with zero prices, private costs are a significant factor in determining household choice. This is particularly true for education, a sector in which opportunity costs make privately borne costs as high as publicly incurred costs of free schooling. Free provision does not mean free consumption. These nonfee costs would cause poor households to demand less education than rich ones. Moreover, the poorest households may choose not to participate at all.

Second, by rationing, many countries have limited the number of people who are allowed access. The impact on efficiency depends crucially upon the rationing scheme's success in detecting those who would benefit the most from the service and upon what sort of behavior the rationing scheme induces.

The most popular method of allocating scarce public school places is by performance on examinations. Although this may appear to select students solely on the basis of ability, in practice it leads to sorting on the basis of willingness to pay. Rich households have more resources than do poor households to invest in tutoring or in materials that prepare their children for these examinations. In African countries such as Mauritius, students are even kept longer in school (through repetition) solely to enhance progression to higher levels of education (Woodhall 1983). The result is an unwarranted overrepresentation of rich households in the rationed school level, which in turn will result in excess investment in schooling inputs that are socially costly and only marginally beneficial in raising productivity. The efficiency loss, then, is substantial. In general, as will be discussed in the "prescriptions" part of this book, a combination of user charges with a loan scheme would ensure efficient allocation.

Piñera and Selowsky (1981) estimate that if the allocation of school places were based more on ability and all the most able students were given the opportunity to benefit from secondary and higher education, the efficiency gains over the current allocation systems would amount to 5 percent of GNP in Latin America, Africa, and the less developed countries of Asia. A more recent study in Colombia concluded that 54 percent of first-year students in tertiary institutions obtained lower scores in aptitude tests than did the corresponding cohort of secondary school graduates who did not attend such institutions (Jimenez 1985).

In curative health, it is not particularly useful to speculate on which type of individual should get priority. Presumably, it is not the individual that matters, but the type of malady; the most serious and life-threatening malady should be given priority treatment.

In health services as in education, it is inefficient to rely solely on prices to determine priority. Diseases or accidents strike randomly and, as will be discussed later, efficient allocation must be based on an insurance scheme that will allow low-income and high-income individuals equal access for similar treatments. Even with insurance schemes, however, it would be efficient to have some fee for payment to deter those who are not in dire need of a service from clogging up the system.

Some anecdotal evidence confirms that short-term excess demand in health has been met by declines in the level of service quality through overcrowding and long waiting lines. World Bank staff have documented instances in which heavily subsidized district hospitals and urban hospital outpatient departments "are swamped with patients" (Mills 1984, 17).

5

Inequities in the Provision of Services

THE SUBSIDIES INHERENT in publicly provided educational and health services have not been equitably distributed. Only a small proportion of the population is able to obtain access to these subsidies. Moreover, the poorest socioeconomic groups are not given priority. Indeed, at least for education subsidies, the richest income groups obtain a disproportionately large share.

The Distribution of Subsidies

Education

A great proportion of government subsidies for education is directed at the highest level. Table 5-1 compares the unit public subsidies for primary, secondary, and higher education. On average over all developing countries, unit subsidies at the higher level are twenty-six times greater than at the primary level and nine times greater than at the secondary level. The discrepancy is largest for the two African regions. At the same time, the proportion of the world regional populations with no education or only primary schooling compared with the proportion with higher education is very small—72 percent versus 6 percent, respectively—as shown in the last four columns of table 5-1.

These figures can be combined to derive a picture of the shares of subsidies acquired by different proportions of the populations (table 5-2). The figures account for the subsidies received by those in higher education throughout their school career, including subsidies at the primary and secondary levels. In the developing countries, 71 percent of the population in each generation receive only primary schooling or less and obtain only 22 percent of the resources devoted to education. The proportion receiving higher education is

52

Table 5-1. Per Student Public Subsidy on Education and Educational Attainment of the Population in Major World Regions, ca. 1980

	\multicolumn{3}{c}{Per student public subsidy as percentage of per capita GNP}	\multicolumn{4}{c}{Enrollment ratio}
Region	Primary education	Secondary education	Higher education	No schooling	Primary education	Secondary education	Higher education
Africa							
Anglophone	18	50	920	23	60	15.8	1.2
Francophone	29	143	804	54	32	11.6	2.4
South Asia	8	18	119	29	52	14.6	4.4
East Asia and Pacific	11	20	118	13	44	33.9	9.1
Latin America	9	26	88	10	46	32.0	12.0
Middle East and North Africa	12	28	150	18	46	26.6	9.4
Developing countries	14	41	370	25	47	22.0	6.0
Developed countries	22	24	49	0	20	59.0	21.0

Source: Based on Mingat and Tan (1985a). Reprinted with permission; copyright 1985 the University of Wisconsin Press.

only 6 percent, but it obtains 39 percent of total resources. In francophone Africa, 2 percent of each cohort in the population attain higher education and receive 40 percent of the public resources devoted to education. In anglophone Africa, 1 percent of the cohort receives more than one-quarter of the public educational resources allotted to it.

The main reason for this disproportionate allocation of resources is the large public reimbursements for out-of-pocket personal costs, such as transport and books (Eicher 1985; Hinchliffe 1985; Mingat and Psacharopoulos 1985). For example, in anglophone Africa, "student subsidies represent 14 percent [of total subsidies] at secondary and higher education levels, while in francophone Africa the figures are much higher, 23 and 43 percent respectively" (Mingat and Psacharopoulos 1985, 36). Also, per student scholarships as a percentage of per capita GNP are 120 percent in the Côte d'Ivoire, 160 percent in Senegal, 700 percent in Mali, and 800 percent in Niger and Burkina Faso.

The rich get a larger proportion of the subsidy because they have more children in school, particularly at those educational levels where subsidies are

Table 5-2. Population and Total Educational Resources by Terminal Level of Schooling in Major World Regions, ca. 1980

	Primary education or less		Higher education	
Region	Population	Resources	Population	Resources
Africa				
Anglophone	83	39	1	26
Francophone	86	16	2	40
South Asia	81	23	4	39
East Asia and Pacific	57	19	9	40
Latin America	56	16	12	42
Middle East and North Africa	64	19	9	45
Developing countries	71	22	6	39
Developed countries	20	8	21	37

Source: Mingat and Tan (1985a). Reprinted with permission; copyright 1985 the University of Wisconsin Press.

highest. The total monetary effect of this on various world regions has recently been estimated by Mingat and Tan (1986a). Table 5-3 shows the proportion of total public resources appropriated for education by different socioeconomic groups. Because of the paucity of income data in developing countries, the distribution figures are categorized on the basis of occupation rather than income. The figures take into account the cumulative effects of subsidies obtained at previous levels of education. A comparison of the share of resources received by three socioeconomic groups with their share of the total population of school-age children provides a measure of the benefit that each socioeconomic group derives from education subsidies. This comparison, which is termed the "subsidy-benefit ratio," is much higher for the white-collar group, indicating that it enjoys a disproportionate share of all education subsidies. In most developing regions, the children of white-collar workers gain nearly six times more benefit from public education subsidies than do the children of farmers. In francophone Africa, the contrast is even more marked—ten to one. Thus, the provision of free or heavily subsidized education does not ensure equity in the distribution of public resources.

Health

Information on the distribution of public health subsidies by income class is even more limited than for education subsidies. Table 5-4 summarizes the

Table 5-3. Public Resources Appropriated for Education by Different Socioeconomic Groups in Major World Regions, ca. 1980

Region	Percentage in the population (1)			Percentage of public school resources (2)			Ratio between proportion of resources and population (2)/(1)		
	Farmers	Manual workers and traders	White-collar workers	Farmers	Manual workers and traders	White-collar workers	Farmers	Manual workers and traders	White-collar workers
Africa									
Anglophone	76	18	6	56	21	23	0.73	1.19	3.78
Francophone	76	18	6	44	21	36	0.58	1.15	5.93
Asia	58	32	10	34	38	28	0.59	1.19	2.79
Latin America	36	49	15	18	51	31	0.49	1.04	2.03
Middle East and North Africa	42	48	10	25	46	29	0.60	0.35	2.87
OECD[a]	12	53	35	11	46	42	0.95	0.87	1.20

a. Organization for Economic Cooperation and Development.
Source: Mingat and Tan (1986a). Reprinted with permission.

Table 5-4. Public Health Subsidies by Income Group in Selected Countries

Country	Survey year	Type of health subsidy	Poorest 20%	20-40%	40-60%	60-80%	80-100%
Chile	1969	Public health	31[b]		35		35[c]
Colombia	1974	National health service	30	23	20	18	12
		Social security system hospital	8	15	29	24	23
		Health center	25	29	23	15	8
		Overall public	20	21	20	20	20
Indonesia	1980	Overall public	19[d]		36[e]		45[c]
Iran, Islamic Rep. of	1977[f]	Overall public	30	21	19	18	13
Malaysia	1974	Inpatient hospital	19	27	10	24	20
		Outpatient hospital	22	20	23	14	6
		Rural clinic	28	27	19	19	8
		Overall public	21	26	15	22	17
Philippines	1975[f]	Overall public	14	13	15	18	40
Sri Lanka	1978[f]	Overall public	25	21	20	19	14

Percentage share by income group[a]

a. All rows sum to approximately 100 percent.
b. Poorest 30 percent income group.
c. Income group 70 to 100 percent.
d. Poorest 40 percent income group.
e. Income group 40 to 70 percent.
f. Year of original study. The figures in this row are quoted from an International Labour Organisation (ILO) review (Richards 1982).

Sources: Foxley, Animat, and Arellano (1979) for Chile; Selowsky (1979) for Colombia; Meesook (1984) for Indonesia; Meerman (1979) for Malaysia; and Richards (1982) for Islamic Republic of Iran, Philippines, and Sri Lanka.

distribution of overall public health subsidies for seven countries. Health subsidy distribution is not as regressive as it is for education. But neither is it progressive, with the possible exception of prerevolutionary Iran; it tends to be neutral. If one adds the first two columns of percentage shares, the poorest 40 percent in Colombia, Malaysia, and Sri Lanka receive, respectively, 41, 47, and 46 percent of the public subsidy for health. This is due mostly to the progressive incidence of public expenditures on rural health care. The distribution is more regressive in Indonesia and the Philippines, where the poorest 40 percent receive only 19 and 27 percent, respectively, of the subsidies from public health centers and hospitals.

The distributions are even more dramatic when one considers the relative needs of income groups. Although space does not permit a thorough review, the bias against lower-income groups in the distribution of public educational and health expenditures is more pronounced when one considers the larger number of school-age children and the incidence of disease for the poorer household.

Overall Distribution of Resources

It is sometimes argued that the regressive distribution of education and health subsidies may be mitigated because most of these subsidies are drawn from general revenues that are financed by a progressive tax system. Although some income tax revenue may be based on a progressive schedule, a large proportion of central government revenue, which funds most health and educational expenditures in highly centralized developing countries, is raised through indirect taxation. Thus, when all sources of tax revenue are taken into account, the tax systems in these countries are not strongly progressive and may even be regressive (see table 5-5).

In summary, the distribution of government subsidies in education and health is, at best, neutral with respect to household income. Indeed, for most types of education the distribution is highly regressive. Thus, current policies regarding the public provision of educational and health services have not succeeded in substantially improving the national distribution of resources.

Reasons for Inequities

Under current pricing arrangements, rich households have greater access to public subsidies in educational and health services than do poor households for several reasons. First, the presence of private costs implies that income constraints limit consumption choices, even if the public authorities do not charge for the services. Second, for any given type of publicly subsidized service, but especially for education, the private costs of using the service are positively related to household income. It is also possible to argue that the private benefits are negatively related to income. Third, among those who are induced to seek the subsidy services, there is excess demand. The methods of rationing scarce services are biased toward the demanders who are rich.

Presence of Private Costs

As stated earlier, free provision is not free consumption. Other costs, such as transport, the purchase of auxiliary complementary services, and the opportunity cost of the consumer's time, are real constraints to poor households.

Table 2-5 indicates the magnitude of nonfee costs for education for selected countries. Although more difficult to estimate directly, the largest nonfee cost, particularly for secondary and higher levels of education, is the opportunity cost of the student's time. This factor is particularly important for education. Many poor households require substantial contributions from children to augment total family resources, especially if work activity is defined as including market work, home production, and housework. For example, in Malaysia the proportion of children in a family participating in work activity rises from 0.31 for Malay girls aged five to six to 0.99 for those

Table 5-5. Taxation by Income Group in Selected Countries, 1970s

	Percentage of income paid in taxes		
Country	Lowest income	Middle income	Highest income
Argentina	17.2	19.8	21.4
Brazil	5.2	14.3	14.8
Chile	18.5	16.2	26.7
Colombia	17.1	13.1	29.9
Kenya	11.5	8.8	12.7
Korea, Rep. of	16.4	15.7	21.6
Lebanon	8.4	20.2	20.3
Malaysia	17.7	16.5	42.1
Mexico	40.2	22.7	14.9
Pakistan	15.0	9.6	25.3
Peru	4.8	17.4	26.6
Philippines	23.0	16.9	33.5

Note: Figures include direct and indirect taxes.
Sources: de Wulf (1975); Foxley, Animat, and Arellano (1979); Gillis and McLure (1978); Heller (1981); and Mann (1982).

aged fifteen to nineteen; and from 0.17 to 0.92, respectively, for Malay boys of the same age groups (de Tray 1984).

Similar costs can be documented for any given type of health service. For example, physician services in the form of government-run clinics may be free, but transport costs would still have to be incurred. Also, drugs may not be subsidized to the same extent (de Ferranti 1983; Musgrove 1983).

These nonfee costs lead poor families in developing countries to demand less of health and educational services than do rich households. If services were completely free and benefits were distributed to all, this demand should be relatively insensitive to income. Moreover, the poorest households may not participate at all. This is particularly true for services, such as education, that are not deemed essential for immediate survival.

Differential Costs and Benefits

It is likely that the costs of consuming any given type of educational or health service are greater and the perceived benefits are less for low-income households. Serving the poorest segments of the population is more costly because they live in sparsely populated rural areas and must bear most of the transport costs, particularly for primary education and primary health care (Jimenez 1986a). The lack of educational credit markets can result in additional costs because the poorest households must choose between savings and present consumption.

Higher-income households perceive the benefits of health and education better than lower-income households do. For educational services, higher-income households tend to provide a better studying environment that includes parental help. This results in increasing returns to education. These households also require an investment vent for their assets when capital markets are constrained. Therefore, they may substitute human for physical capital in their investment portfolio.

Inequitable distribution of resources also occurs because spending for urban schools far outstrips that for rural schools. Table 5-6 illustrates this trend, which is most pronounced for postprimary education. In rural areas of Colombia, where 32 percent of the school-age population reside, secondary education receives 19 percent of total government resources. In rural areas of Indonesia, where 76 percent of the school-age population reside, lower secondary education receives 50 percent of the government subsidies.

Similar inequities apply to the health sector. According to table 5-7, rural populations in China receive 29 percent of all government subsidies but comprise 79 percent of the total population.

Table 5-6. Government Education Subsidy by Type of Education and Location in Selected Countries

Country	Year	Type of education	Percentage share of educational subsidy – Rural	Percentage share of educational subsidy – Urban	Percentage share of school-age cohort – Rural	Percentage share of school-age cohort – Urban
Indonesia	1982	Primary	83	17	84	16
		Upper secondary	71	29	80	20
		Lower secondary	50	50	76	23
		University	21	79	78	22
		All levels	76	24	83	17
Malaysia[a]	1974	Primary	52	48	—	—
		Secondary	50	50	—	—
		Postsecondary	37	63	—	—
		All levels	—	—	56	44
Colombia	1974	Primary	35	65	35	65
		Secondary	19	81	32	68
Kenya[b]	1976	Secondary	87	13	95	5

— Not available.

Note: Rural and urban figures for each country total 100 percent.

a. Shares are estimated from enrollment in public institutions. Shares of school-age cohort are assumed to be equivalent to population shares.

b. Urban shares are from enrollment data on assisted schools in Nairobi.

Sources: Meesook (1984) for Indonesia; Meerman (1979) for Malaysia; Selowsky (1979) for Colombia; and Bertrand and Griffin (1983) for Kenya.

Rationing

Because there is excess demand for most subsidized social services, the distribution of public spending on them depends not only on which types of households want them, but also on how the public authority decides to allocate scarce school places or hospital beds.

For educational services, the allocation methods tend to be regressive. The most common way of rationing scarce educational places is by examination: those with the highest scores are allowed to enter. This approach may be efficient, but it is not necessarily equitable. Even if it is assumed that innate ability is randomly distributed throughout the population, children from rich households can be expected to do better on examinations than those from poor groups. Rich parents can spend more on books and private tutoring, and they are more likely to encourage studying. (The impact of socioeconomic

Table 5-7. **Government Health Subsidy by Type of Service and Location in Selected Countries**

Country	Year	Type of service	Percentage share of government subsidy Rural	Urban	Percentage share of population Rural	Urban
Indonesia[a]	1983	All public (Java)[b]	50	16	55	11
		All public (Outer)[b]	27	6	28	6
		All public	77	23	83	17
Malaysia[c]	1974	All public	57	43	60	40
Senegal	1981–82	All public	57	43[d]	81	19[d]
Colombia	1974	National health services hospitals	39	61	—	—
		Social security hospitals	2	98	—	—
		Health clinics	23	77	—	—
		All public	19	81	38	62
China	1981	Hospitals[e]	25	75	—	—
		Other Ministry of Public Health activities	84	16	—	—
		Medical insurance[f]	0	100	—	—
		All public	29	71	79	21

— Not available.
Note: Subsidies are government expenditures less any fees received.
a. Services include government hospitals, public health centers, and community health volunteers.
b. Percentages of all Indonesia subsidies.
c. Services include government, district, and general hospitals; public health centers; community health volunteers; and rural outpatient clinics.
d. For Cap Vert region (Dakar).
e. Expenditures by the Ministry of Public Health. Services include hospitals of traditional medicine, commune health centers, and antiepidemic activities.
f. Expenditures by the Ministry of Finance to provide free health care.
Sources: Meesook (1984) for Indonesia; Meerman (1979) for Malaysia; Selowsky (1979) for Colombia; Prescott and Jamison (1984) for China; and de Ferranti (1983) for all others.

characteristics on school achievement is well documented; see, for example, Heyneman and Loxley 1983). To get good grades or to pass competitive tests, children often must repeat a year of schooling—an expense poor households are less able to afford. These discrepancies are greater by the time students reach higher education, where selectivity is most stringent. How this selection affected school authorities and the students themselves is illustrated in a

Colombian case study (Jimenez 1985). More than half of the tertiary-level students scored lower in aptitude tests than did the nonstudents. These low-scoring students come from higher-income families.

For health services, the rationing system varies considerably by type of service. For publicly provided curative care, rationing is typically by queue. The distributional impact of queues is unclear: if opportunity costs are lower for poor households, they may be progressive. For poor people seeking public services, however, wages lost by time off work could impair their ability to survive; with such a high opportunity cost, queues could be very regressive.

Changing Pricing Policy

6

Basic Principles Revisited

THE PREVIOUS CHAPTERS have documented the current state of pricing policy in education and health. In general, prices are uniformly low for most publicly provided services. Given the budgetary constraints confronting many national governments, the efficiency and equity of this policy have been questioned.

This chapter reviews the economic principles on which policy options can be based to improve efficiency and equity. In the succeeding two chapters, these principles are applied to educational and health services.

Pricing Policy for Efficient Provision

In economics, the allocation of resources in providing educational and health services has been treated differently from other goods and services. Standard economic rules regarding efficiency pricing do not apply for the reasons outlined in the last section of chapter 2. Many educational and health services are characterized by externalities, scale economies, "merit goods" arguments, and nonexclusivity. Because these characteristics have been used to justify public intervention in private markets, they have been called "public goods" characteristics.

These features, however, do not imply that pricing should have no role at all in mobilizing resources to provide educational and health services or in determining who should obtain access to them. Indeed, the previous three chapters have argued that extremely low or zero prices across all services, whether implicitly applied or explicitly decreed, have substantial costs in terms of efficiency and equity. First, not all educational services or all health services are alike. Some, such as primary education or immunization programs, are characterized by positive externalities, whereas others, such as higher education or outpatient curative care, are not. The same can be said for the other characteristics mentioned above. Second, even if a service exhibited these characteristics, it does not necessarily mean that pricing principles should be ignored. Rather, standard pricing rules should be adapted to fit any given situation.

In addition to public goods characteristics, current private demand determines whether pricing in resource mobilization and allocation is efficient. If there is excess private demand, the scope for raising prices would obviously be greater; if not, consumption would be affected by price changes, depending upon the responsiveness of private demand to changes in price. This responsiveness can be measured empirically as the price elasticity of demand, which is the percentage change in quantity demanded for a given percentage change in price. If this magnitude exceeds one, demand is considered relatively elastic. If it is less than one, demand is considered relatively inelastic.

Policy Tools

When utilization of a service is low, its marginal benefit is high. For example, when there are few secondary school graduates, the productive contribution of another graduate is relatively large. As utilization rises, marginal benefits fall. The most socially desirable or optimal level of consumption (denoted as q^* in this book) is the level at which the additional gain to society from another unit of consumption is equal to the additional cost. For example, the optimal enrollment ratio in secondary school is 75 percent if, when three-fourths of the relevant age group are enrolled, the gain to society of educating another secondary student does not outweigh the cost of doing so. So, it is not worth educating that "marginal" youngster, and present enrollment ratios must be optimal.

According to the evidence presented in chapter 3, most societies have yet to reach these optimal levels for most social services. Therefore, expansion is worthwhile. The policy question is how to finance these services. Governments have several pricing options: they can fully subsidize these services, charge fees for them, or choose a combination of fees and subsidies. The optimal policy is the combination of prices and subsidy that induces users to demand q^* and that is also sufficient to finance q^*. The optimal level of fees depends upon the characteristics of the service and upon private demand.

Subsidy, or budgetary, allocations (S) and unit prices (p) are treated separately in this discussion for two reasons. First, subsidy and price levels are two policy tools that can be independently adjusted by governmental authorities. Second, prices and subsidy allocations are frequently determined by separate governmental bodies. For example, a ministry of finance may set subsidy allocation levels, while ministries of health or education may determine the prices charged to those who use public health and educational facilities.

Nevertheless, prices and subsidy allocations are closely linked. Together, they determine the unit subsidy (s). Governments must try to adjust both simultaneously in order to set the appropriate level of generated health and educational services. Frequently, this is not done, and underinvestment in human capital results.

If c symbolizes the unit cost of providing a social service,[1] then a simple formula for financing the optimal level of consumption would be

$$cq^* = S + pq^*.$$

The expression implies a unit subsidy,

$$s \equiv S/q^* = c - p.$$

Both prices (p) and subsidy allocations (S) can be manipulated to produce the optimal outcome. At times, however, at least one may be constrained at a certain level. If one is set too low, the other policy tool must be allowed to adjust upward to provide q^*. Otherwise, there will be underinvestment. Since the cost of using general tax revenue to subsidize health or educational services is the forgone expenditure on other types of social services, the level of subsidies (S) available for health or education may be fixed.[2] This rigidity is reinforced if the level of subsidies is determined by one agency (such as the finance ministry), while pricing policy is set by another (such as the education or health ministry).

Case 1: High Externalities

Tight budget constraints imply that the total subsidy allocation, together with whatever private payments are collected in the form of fees, may be insufficient to finance q^*. This has recently been reflected in the understatement of recurrent costs, especially prevalent in education, health, and other social sectors (see Heller and Cheasty 1984).

In this situation, with a fixed subsidy allocation, S, the appropriate policy response would be to raise prices. If the revenue thereby raised is used to increase the supply of the service, then expansion—closer to the socially op-

---

1. In the notation of chapter 2, unit cost c may be considered as the sum of recurrent cost (rc) and annualized capital cost (cc) to the government.
2. This analysis assumes that there is no difference in the costs of administering the subsidy or the pricing policy. Administration costs are discussed later.

timal level—would be allowed. But by how much should prices be raised? The best policy in this case would be to raise prices to clear the market, as long as consumption still has not reached q^*. This rule is extremely useful since, to determine the magnitude of the price change that is socially efficient, it is not necessary to observe the entire marginal social benefit schedule. Calculating excess demand or supply is sufficient.[3] Thobani (1983) examined this case for education in Malawi.

Case 2: Low Externalities and Excess Demand

With services that do not exhibit strong public goods characteristics and for which there is currently excess demand, price increases should obviously be greater. The appropriate extent of the increase depends partly on how the additional resources that are generated will be spent.

If additional revenues are restricted to being spent on the same service, then prices should be raised to generate only enough resources to finance the socially optimal amount of consumption, q^*. At this price level, excess demand is likely, since a substantial subsidy allocation (S) is already being provided. This excess demand should not be met. Rather, it would be efficient to ration the service.

If intrasectoral reallocations of the total funds available are possible, then prices should be raised to the marginal willingness to pay at q^*. The resources thus generated, however, should be used to expand the service that has the highest social returns. This means that resources generated in one subsector (say, higher education) may be spent in another (say, primary education). They can even be used to stimulate demand for other services for which there is little private demand but high social returns.

---

3. What is important is agreement concerning the socially optimal level of consumption, q^*. Without this consensus, it would not be possible to determine whether the level at which the subsidy is fixed is greater or less than S^*. Indeed, if it were greater than S^*, it would be socially efficient either to have a price low enough to reduce excess demand (if all of the subsidies and private payments were used to finance the system) or to have the school system save the excess subsidy to prevent the utilization of the system beyond q^*. Thus, market characteristics could not be used to determine the magnitude of the price drop if the system were initially in excess supply or even the direction of the price change if the system were initially in excess demand. To determine q^*, policymakers must agree on the level of consumption at which the marginal social benefit of another unit of educational service is equal to its marginal social cost. The level of q^* is probably much less than the target levels set by broad objectives such as universal access to education or health care, since they do not ordinarily take costs into account.

Case 3: High Externalities but Weak Private Demand

For some services, private costs may be so high that even at zero prices there is no demand. Yet social benefits may be high for services such as primary education or health care in rural areas. Prices should then be made even lower—that is, they should be negative. Subsidy allocations should be increased for these services. Subsidies can take several forms: direct transfers to stimulate demand, rebates to cover privately incurred costs, or service expansion that would lower travel costs. The mode of transfer would depend on whether the service is a merit good. If households are not aware of the full benefits of the service, then it would be better to reimburse cost rather than augment income.

A Graphic Presentation

Cases 1, 2, and 3 are summarized succinctly in demand and supply figures 6-1, 6-2, and 6-3, respectively. In figure 6-1, the curvilinear line S represents the relationship between the prices charged by the government and the amount the government can provide, given its unit cost, cc_p, and a fixed sub-

Figure 6-1. Pricing with High Externalities under a Budgetary Constraint

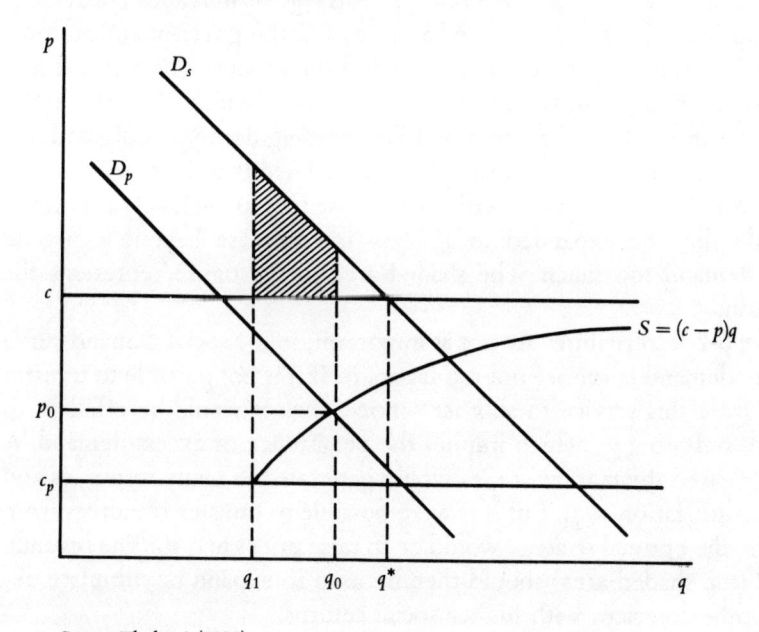

Source: Thobani (1983).

Figure 6-2. Pricing with Low Externalities and Excess Demand

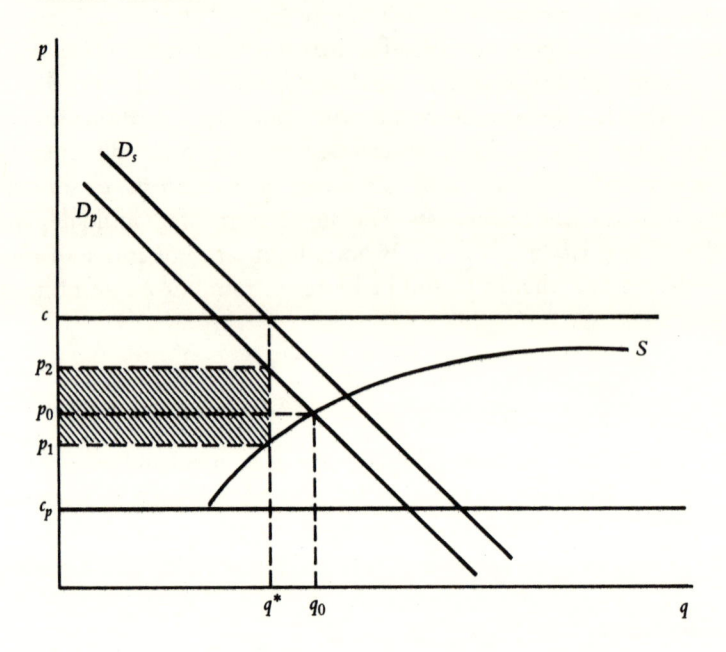

sidy allocation S. For example, at a zero price, the government can provide q_1 and the implied unit subsidy is cc_p. At a price $p_0 c_p$, the government can provide q_0, if the price revenue is used to expand the service. The implied unit subsidy is $c p_0$. If the subsidy allocation is fixed at S, which Thobani (1983) calls the iso-subsidy line, the curve will be a rectangular hyperbola with respect to c. For simplicity in this example, it is assumed that the service is provided for free. Thus, it would be efficient to raise fees to the level p_0. The service should then be expanded to q_0. Any fee increase beyone p_0 would constrain demand too much. The shaded area in the figure represents the welfare gain.

In figure 6-2, externalities are not as important, so the social demand curve and private demand curve are not too far apart. If it is not possible to transfer resources from this service to another service, then it would be efficient to raise prices only to $c_p p_1$, which implies the persistence of excess demand. A price that cleared the market at $c_p p_0$ would generate too many resources and lead to overutilization at q_0. But if it were possible to transfer resources from this service, the optimal strategy would be to raise prices to $c_p p_2$. The revenue generated (the shaded area) should then be used to expand or stimulate demand for other services with higher social returns.

Figure 6-3 depicts private costs that are so high that even with zero prices private demand is not strong enough to use up all the resources that are avail-

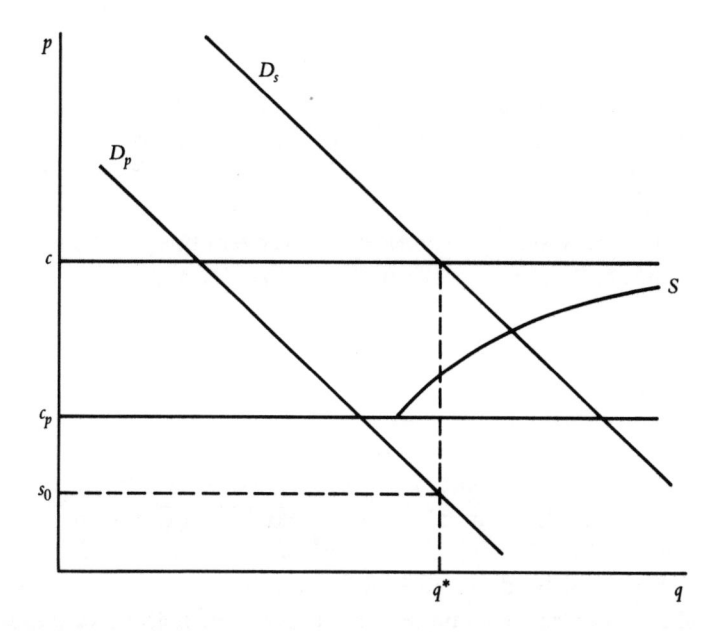

Figure 6-3. Pricing with High Externalities but Weak Private Demand

able through the subsidy allocation. The optimal strategy would be to use additional subsidies—not to expand the service, but to stimulate demand. This would cause the private demand curve, D_p, to shift out to D_s. Prices could then be levied. Alternatively, they could be used to subsidize the individual consumer and lower the private costs. The amount of the subsidy (or negative price) would be the amount $c_p s_0$.

Pricing Policy for Efficient and Equitable Access

Increased prices, while mobilizing the resources required to expand educational and health services with high rates of return, may have negative side effects, particularly on the efficiency and equity of access.

Even with zero or negligible prices, the presence of substantial private costs can mean an inefficient and inequitable distribution of educational and health subsidies (see chapter 4). Much of this is due to the uniformly low prices charged for services with different public goods characteristics. Thus, charging higher prices for some services, such as higher education and outpatient curative health care, while keeping low the prices of other services, such as primary education or health care, would lead to improvements in social welfare. Such a policy, however, would further restrict access to those services where higher prices are charged. After all, it would be beneficial to ensure that poor people have access to higher education. And to mitigate the effects of such restrictions, it would be efficient and equitable to introduce discriminatory pricing.

Discriminatory prices for services should take into account the characteristics of the users. To ensure efficiency, priority should be given to those who would benefit the most: in education, those with the highest innate ability; in health, those who are the most infirm. Because income is presumably uncorrelated with innate ability or the probability of getting sick, it would be inefficient, if financial markets do not work well, to base access only on willingness to pay. How should policymakers circumvent this problem? They can target subsidies, and they can assist in developing the appropriate financial market.

Targeting Subsidies

To the extent that subsidies are warranted because of externalities or because capital markets do not work well, they should be distributed by discriminating among individuals. In education, it would be efficient to have a merit-based scheme that ensured access to those who are the most able academically. This could be done by limiting access according to achievement in school or on entrance examinations. Because of high private costs, however, it would be insufficient to simply accept students on the basis of scores. Scholarships ought to be distributed to the meritorious who are also needy, but not to those who can afford to pay.

In health, it would be efficient to have a system that distinguished among those who need care the most. Subsidies should also be restricted to the needy, since others would be willing and able to pay for the services they require.

The most troublesome aspect of such discrimination is that it is costly to implement. Many governments find it difficult to rank individuals or households by income. In developed countries, such an exercise would be facilitated by relying on the income tax system, which is calibrated to discriminate among individuals. In less developed countries, the tax system is not sophisticated enough to allow the use of tax returns, although less formal ways of discriminating among individuals are frequently available. (In Pakistan, for example, teachers report on students' availability for scholarships.) Thus, for services that are distributed on a large scale, the costs of discriminating by individual may be too large. But for services that are limited to a small segment of the population (such as hospital-based health care or university education), the costs may not be too onerous.

Even if the costs of discriminating by individual or by household are too large, it may be efficient to discriminate by groups of individuals. For example, in most countries, prices charged for primary education and health care in urban and rural areas are uniformly low (see chapter 4). At the very least, it would be manageable to discriminate on the basis of geography—lower prices in poor rural areas and higher prices in urban areas.

Many have argued that it is better to charge uniformly low prices; entry restrictions could then be used to limit access to appropriate individuals, if budgetary restraints prevented all demand from being met. Such restrictions could give priority to those applicants who value the service the most. But in practice they would also have the following adverse repercussions. First, many poor households must be induced to apply because of high private costs. Second, as indicated in chapter 3, a main problem is the need to generate additional resources for the social sectors. Although a well-functioning rationing scheme would have the same efficiency effects as a pricing scheme in terms of discriminating for access, there would be underinvestment. Third, quantity rationing schemes may induce users to behave inefficiently. For example, if the rationing scheme were achievement on an entrance exam or in school, there would be incentives to overinvest in education.

Making Financial Markets Work

Another way to ensure access and lower the need for subsidies would be to assist the financial market. In education, student loans would encourage educational investments by enabling students and their families to finance current studies out of expected future income. Thus, if the returns to education are high, the provision of student loans would further increase the flow of private resources into education. It would also result in a better selection of students, since the competition for places and living expenses would no longer be limited to individuals whose families could afford tuition and living expenses at the time of enrollment.

In health, insurance would mitigate the risks of potentially high expenditures on hospital and physician services. Thus, care would not be limited only to those who have cash on hand. It would be inefficient to make all households finance these expenses out of savings, even if they had them. Instead, households should put their savings in the most productive investment and pay only a small premium for the insurance.

Some form of government involvement in loan and insurance programs, either as a provider or guarantor of funds, is usually needed. The risk and cost of lending to students or insuring for high hospital payments may be too large for private banks to absorb without prohibitive increases in interest charges. The government, however, would be large enough to absorb such risks without having to incur the transactions costs of obtaining detailed in-

A Graphic Presentation

Figure 6-4 depicts the gains from price discrimination. Suppose that for one group of individuals (I), social benefits exceed private benefits (for example, the poor do not have access to financial markets). Thus, the social demand curve D_s exceeds the private demand curve D_p (see figure 6-4A). For the other group of individuals (II), social and private benefits are the same, so that D_s equals D_p (see figure 6-4B). In this case, a uniform subsidy implied by, say, a zero price would be inefficient. It would cause underutilization of the amount $q_1 q_0$ by I and overutilization of the amount $q_3 \, q_2$ by II. This uniform price policy would be inferior to a policy that provided a direct payment $c_p \, t_0$ to a type I individual to increase the unit subsidy and charged a price of $c_p \, c$ to an individual of type II. The welfare gains of the latter policy over a uniform price policy are represented by areas ABD plus EFG.

A differential pricing scheme is superior to a completely quantity-based rationing scheme that maintained a zero price and rationed q to q_3 for type II individuals. First, although the appropriate amount of consumption by type II individuals is induced, type I individuals would still underconsume at q_1. Second, if there is a problem with resource mobilization—a problem confronting most developing countries—provision of the service for either type I or type II individuals would not be adequate. An increase in prices would mobilize resources within the sector. Third, when goods or services are rationed, those who have access to the service obtain "economic rents." In other words, because they are subsidized and pay less than the true economic value of the service, they are better off than those who are not selected. In figure 6-4B, the value of these rents would be $cEHc_p$. The competition of these rents could result in socially unproductive activities.

Technical Note

The impact of policy changes on key variables can be roughly estimated. This would require the specification of the demand and supply systems depicted in figures 6-1 to 6-4. The equations are summarized here since they will be used in the succeeding chapters. The general reader can skip this section without loss of continuity.

To simplify the analysis, demand (q^d) is assumed to be a log-linear function of the cost of consumption (including fees, p, directly incurred private costs, dpc, and opportunity costs, oc) and of other variables (A):

Figure 6-4. Welfare Gains from Price Discrimination

A. Type I Individuals
(social benefits exceed private benefits; optimal user charge equals $-c_p t_0$)

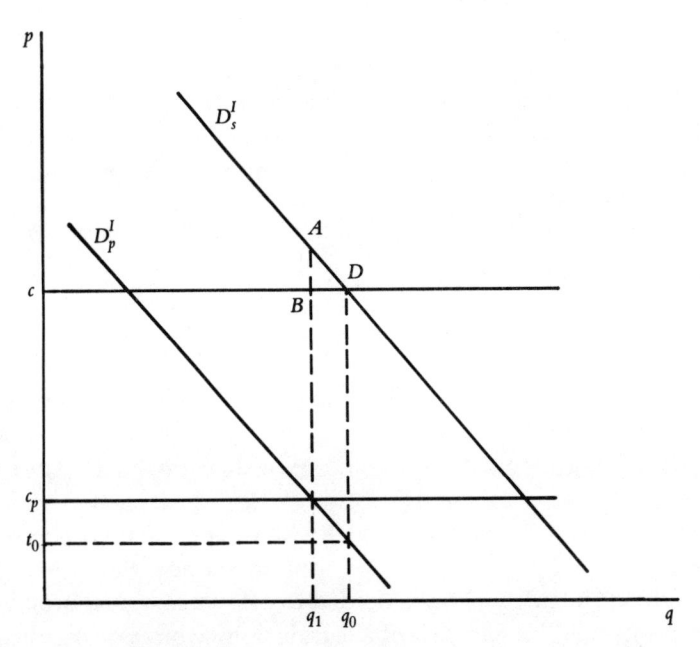

B. Type II Individuals
(social benefits equal private benefits; optimal user charge equals cc_p)

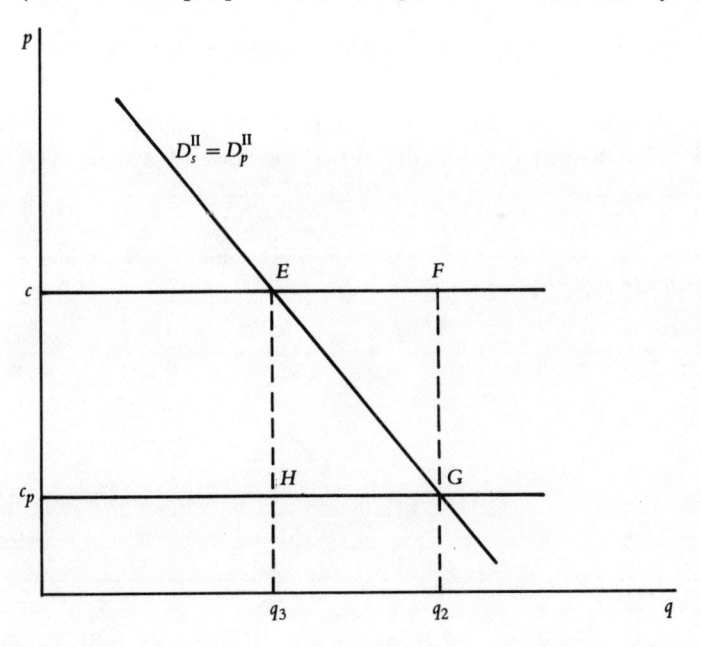

$$(6\text{-}1) \qquad q^d = A\,(p + dpc + oc)^\alpha$$

where α is interpreted to be the elasticity of demand with respect to all private costs. The fee elasticity of demand (η) is this magnitude times that share of fees in all private costs.[4] The elasticity of demand with respect to other cost components is an analogous expression.

The total cost of providing a service is the unit cost of providing it (c) times the quantity provided (q). The total cost is financed by private payments to the provider (pq) and a lump-sum subsidy allocation by the government (S), which can be expressed in symbols as

$$(6\text{-}2) \qquad (c - p)q = S.$$

In the disequilibrium models of the figures, the amount that is provided is constrained by the demand equation (6-1) in cases where there is no excess demand and by the government budget constraint (6-2) in cases of excess demand. If the equilibrium (market-clearing) price and quantity are p_0 and q_0 (obtained by solving for them in 6-1 and 6-2), then $q = S/(c-p)$ for $q < q_0$, and $q = A(p + dpc + oc)\alpha$ for $q > q_0$.

In appendix C, a more general model is developed that can be used to determine (1) the marginal impact of a drop in subsidy allocations (S) on utilization (q); (2) the price increase needed to offset a marginal drop in subsidy allocations; and (3) the impact of a marginal price increase on utilization and overall household payments. For example, under the assumption of excess demand, the magnitude of (1) is

$$(6\text{-}3) \qquad \partial q/\partial S = 1/[c(e + 1) - p]$$

where e is the unit cost elasticity with respect to the amount of the services provided. The magnitudes for the other expressions are derived in appendix C.

---

4. Differentiating equation 6-1 with respect to p and multiplying the resulting expression by (p/q^d) yields $(p/q^d)(\partial q^d/\partial p) = \eta = \alpha p/(p + dpc + oc)$.

7

Changing Pricing Policy in Education

THE PREVIOUS CHAPTERS have argued that prices should be given a greater role in the mobilization of resources to expand some types of educational and health services. Such a policy was recommended because of its potential for improving both efficiency and equity. In these last two chapters, the possible effects of such a policy in education and health are considered.

An increase in user charges is warranted for educational services that do not exhibit "public goods" characteristics, such as externalities, and for which private demand is strong at current prices. Externalities lessen with the level of education. Thus, the case for greater cost recovery through pricing can be made for higher (postsecondary) and urban-based secondary education. In primary education, externalities are important. But if budget restraints inhibit the increase of subsidies to that level and if private demand is strong enough (as it often is in urban areas), then a case can also be made for greater cost recovery for primary education. The applicability of user charges can be roughly categorized on the basis of some general characteristics of levels of education (see table 7-1). These conclusions may vary in specific cases because of country conditions.

Behavioral Parameters

Before estimating the magnitude of the impact of increased user charges, we need to review the literature on the parameters of demand and supply that will affect the calculations. Then the greater role of user charges at various levels of education, as well as accompanying policies, can be discussed in more quantitative terms. The most important parameters are those that govern preference and cost: how demand is likely to vary with respect to price changes and how cost is likely to vary with changes in scale.

Table 7-1. Stylized Market Characteristics of Educational Services

Level of education	"Public good" characteristic	Market for places at at current prices
Higher	Lack of capital market	Excess demand
Secondary		
Urban	Lack of capital market	Excess demand
Rural	Lack of capital market; inadequate knowledge of benefits	Excess supply
Primary		
Urban	Externalities	Excess demand
Rural	Externalities; inadequate knowledge of benefits	Excess supply

The Responsiveness of Demand

Families must make many decisions about education. Should their children go to school? If so, should all their children go, or should some remain at home? How much education should they have? And is academic schooling better than vocational training? The answers to these questions depend upon several variables, among them the cost of obtaining the education.

The price responsiveness of educational demand is reflected in the price elasticity, which measures the percentage change in demand with respect to a 1 percent change in the price charged to the user of the educational service. Most demand studies are not able to measure price changes accurately. Some countries do not change prices at all, and those that do, vary them very slightly, which makes it difficult to observe behavioral responses to price variation. Since price is not the only cost-related variable that affects demand, however, most studies are able to use variations in directly incurred private costs or opportunity costs to infer behavioral parameters. When weighed by the share of price in total private costs, these elasticities can be interpreted as reasonable proxies for price elasticity (see table 7-2). The differences in the measures of demand (including household spending on education, the probability of having one child in school, and enrollment ratios) reflect the various choices that families make about schooling.

The measures of private costs used in table 7-2 also vary. Some are indirect measures, such as household size. A greater number of children enrolled implies higher costs of educating an additional child and thus a lower enrollment ratio among children in the household, if income is held constant (Birdsall 1980; Mingat, Tan, and Hoque 1984). Other measures that are used include distance to school and mean wages (opportunity costs) for children of different age groups.

Despite the variability in these measures, an increase in most components of private costs would result in a less than proportionate decrease in the demand for education.[1] This conclusion can certainly be extended to fees since fees can be expected to be an even smaller proportion of total private costs. In the analysis that follows, the effects of alternative assumptions about fee elasticity are simulated.

Another way to estimate changes in demand would be to calculate the impact of increased user charges on the perceived private rate of return to education. If this rate of return were to drop below that of investment in alternative activities, the family would be expected to stop investing in education. Table 7-3 presents the effects of price increases on primary and secondary school enrollment in Malawi. It is based upon the response of primary and secondary students who were asked whether they would drop out of school if certain fees were increased. The percentage declines in enrollment listed in column 3 are likely to be overstated since respondents, who would rather not pay a higher fee, have an incentive to understate their private rate of return. Despite this potential bias, the responsiveness of potential enrollment is not very large in comparison with fee changes. At the secondary level, the percentage drop in enrollment is not substantially larger than the percentage fee increase. At higher fee increases, the former is smaller than the latter. At the primary level, the percentage drop in enrollment is half or less than half the percentage increase in price.[2]

In April 1982, the Malawian government did in fact increase school fees. The increase varied between urban and rural areas and by type of school. At the primary level an increase in fees of 45 to 50 percent produced a mean drop-out rate of 1.4 to 1.7 percent, respectively, while at the secondary level an increase of 50 to 150 percent produced a drop-out rate of 4.3 to 7.8 percent, respectively (Tan, Lee, and Mingat 1984, table 8).

The Responsiveness of Cost

The level of public educational services depends upon the willingness and the ability of the public authorities to provide them. An inquiry into bureau-

---

1. Of all the studies cited in table 7-2, only one (Taiwan), which uses economywide time series data and is likely fraught with aggregation bias, computes an elasticity that exceeds one.

2. It would, of course, be misleading to infer the magnitude of the fee elasticity of demand from these data since elasticity is defined as percentage changes in demand with respect to very small changes in price.

Table 7-2. Price and Income Elasticities of Demand for Education

	Level of analysis	Latest year of data	Dependent variable	Income measure	Price measure	Income	Price
						\multicolumn{2}{c}{Elasticities}
Colombia	Household	1967–68	Spending on education	Husband's income	Household characteristics (number of children of different age groups)	1.045	Inelastic
			Share of household budget on education			0.334	Inelastic
			Actual expenditures/ predicted expenditures			1.035	Inelastic
			Household education achievement index			1.343	Inelastic
El Salvador	Household	1980	Spending on education	Household permanent income (proxied by expenditure)	Household characteristics	...	...
Santa Ana						0.967	Inelastic
Sonsonate						0.023	Inelastic
Malawi	Household	1983	Household enrollment ratio	Father's income	Total household cost	...	−0.52

Malaysia	Household	1976	Population of school-children	Household income	Distance to secondary school	0.097	−0.039
			Age 6-11			0.318	−0.012
			Age 12-18				
Mali	Household	1982	Enrollment ratio	Household income	Fees to parent association	...	−0.98
					Distance to school	...	−0.26
					Quality (availability of books)	...	0.14
Pakistan	Individual	1978–79	Probability of going to school	Household income per capita	...	0.01 to 0.15	...
Philippines	Individual	1968	Years of completed schooling	Father's wage in 1968	Mean wage for children		
					Age 7-14	0.111	−0.05
					Age 15-19	0.111	−0.008
Taiwan	Countrywide time series	1950–69	Number taking college entrance exam	Per capita income	Average tuition and fees	0.383	1.763
Tanzania	Individual	1981	Spending on education	Father's income	...	0.03	...

... Information not provided by the study.

Sources: Birdsall (1980) for Colombia; World Bank data for El Salvador; Tan, Lee, and Mingat (1984) for Malawi; de Tray (1984) for Malaysia; Birdsall (1983a) for Mali; Lucas (1984) for Pakistan; King and Lillard (1983) for Philippines; Kondrassis and Tseng (1976) for Taiwan; and Tan (1985a) for Tanzania.

Table 7-3. Percentage of Malawian Students Expecting to Leave School after Hypothetical Increase in Fees, 1983

Level of education	Fee after increase (kwacha) (1)	Increase as percentage of total fee (2)	Percentage decline in enrollment (3)	(3)/(2) (4)
Primary	10	48	−22	−0.46
(cost recovery	20	196	−38	−0.19
K16 per student)	30	344	−18	−0.14
	50	640	−57	−0.09
Secondary	40	33	−52	−1.58
(cost recovery	60	100	−75	−0.75
K266 per student)	100	233	−85	−0.36
	200	567	−91	−0.16

Note: GNP per capita in 1982 was approximately 219 kwacha (K) according to International Monetary Fund statistics.

Source: Calculated from Tan, Lee, and Mingat (1984), table 4.

cratic behavior, however, is beyond the scope of this book. It is assumed here that government provision of education is consistent with a search for social efficiency—an economical and equitable allocation of resources.

Education can be financed out of government subsidies and collected fees. Increased fees obviously strengthen the ability of public authorities to provide educational services. But collected fees are not always earmarked for education; they may be treated like general tax revenue. In this section, however, all user fees are assumed to be kept within the education sector except when noted otherwise. The maximum amount of educational service that can be provided would therefore be the sum of the total subsidy and user charge revenue, divided by the unit cost. The education cost structure could thus influence the impact of user charges.

Although not comprehensive, some evidence in developing countries suggests that the average costs of providing education decline as enrollment increases—that is, that there are economies of scale. According to a study of average costs and enrollment ratios that was based on aggregate data from eighty-three countries, an increase of the higher education enrollment ratio from 1 percent to 2 percent would lower average costs by 15 percent (Psacharopoulos 1982). This magnitude is much less for greater enrollment ratios. An increase of the higher education enrollment ratio from 10 percent to 11 percent would lower average costs by only 6 percent. The same cross-national study also compiled within-country estimates (see table 7-4). The qualitative results do not change. An annual increment in enrollment of about

Table 7-4. Changes in Enrollment in Higher Education
and Average Cost per Student, Selected Periods
(percent)

Country	Period	Enrollment change	Real cost change
Egypt	1957–75	9.5	0.2
Ghana	1957–75	8.2	−9.2
Kenya	1968–70	20.4	−10.9
Mexico	1961–75	13.0	−0.8
Pakistan	1964–75	8.4	−6.3
Thailand	1954–64	6.4	0.1
Zambia	1969–73	21.5	−8.6
Average		12.5	−5.1

Source: Psacharopoulos (1982).

12 percent is associated with a fall of 5 percent in unit cost. This represents a total cost elasticity of 1.4.[3]

At the primary and secondary levels, there are only a few within-country studies that utilize microlevel data. The elasticity of cost with respect to a marginal primary student in Bolivia is 0.59 and in Paraguay, 0.5; for a marginal secondary student in Bolivia it is 0.54 (Jimenez 1986a). These findings also suggest the presence of scale economies.

Prices and Expansion

As was shown in table 7-1, user charges are more appropriate for higher education and perhaps for the secondary level than for primary education, presuming that financial markets can be made to work better. The gains from user charges will be discussed in terms of expansion, efficiency, and equity for all three levels.

Higher Education

When education budgets are limited and the available subsidy is insufficient to fund the optimal amount of schooling, efficiency will be improved by increasing user fees and using the revenue to expand those levels of educa-

---

3. In this context it should be kept in mind that there is only limited evidence on the elasticity of demand for higher education in developing countries, and differences in elasticities across income groups and for different price levels could not be estimated.

tion with the highest social rates of return. The feasibility of mobilizing sufficient resources depends upon the responsiveness of demand and supply. If there is excess demand, prices can be raised to mobilize revenue until equilibrium is restored. Beyond that point, the ability to mobilize resources depends upon the elasticity of demand. If demand is relatively price inelastic, the percentage amount by which consumption drops will be less than the percentage increase in prices, and there will be a revenue gain.

Heavy unit subsidies for higher education, at a time when budgets are constrained, have led to excess demand in many countries. In Nigeria, for example, the average acceptance rate for university education was only 16 percent in 1979–80, and in some specialties, such as business administration and law, it was even as low as 8 and 5 percent, respectively (Hinchliffe 1985). In Indonesia, on average only 30 percent of all applicants to institutions of higher education were accommodated in the early 1980s (Hanovice 1984). In several Latin American countries, there is evidence the number of applications for university education exceeds the available places by a factor of at least two (Schiefelbein 1985). Further evidence of the insufficiency of local facilities to meet the private demand for higher education is the large and growing number of developing country nationals studying abroad (Lee and Tan 1984). For example, in Greece one out of every four postsecondary students attends a foreign institution, often with family financial support.

In cases where there is excess demand, revenue will increase by the amount of the increase in user charges. Once the demand has been satisfied, the amount of revenue generated will depend upon demand elasticities, as explained in the previous chapter. Where should the resources be spent? They should be spent where the social rates of return are highest. In most cases, this means primary education.

Table 7-5 shows the potential efficiency gains of expanding primary education through increased private contributions to higher education in twelve African countries. By shifting the financial responsibility for living allowances from governments to students or their families, enough public resources would be freed to allow, on average, an 18 percent expansion of the yearly primary education budget. These additional funds would allow greater coverage of the primary-school-aged population. An additional expansion of 23 percent in the primary school budget would be possible if fees recovered all operating costs in higher education. Thus, if both kinds of subsidies in higher education were fully withdrawn, the primary education budget would be expanded, on average, by about 40 percent.

The expansionary effect differs from country to country.[4] In Côte d'Ivoire, Malawi, Senegal, Sudan, Tanzania, and Togo, the potential expan-

4. Unit costs are assumed to be constant in these calculations.

Table 7-5. **Potential Increase in Primary Education Budget Financed by Raising Higher Education Fees in Selected African Countries, 1980**

	Higher education fees raised to recover		
Country	Living expenses	Operating costs	Both
Benin	18.9	5.0	23.9
Burkina Faso	18.6	8.0	26.6
Central African Republic	12.4	4.0	16.4
Congo, People's Republic of the	17.6	5.8	23.4
Côte d'Ivoire	21.0	19.2	40.2
Malawi	8.6	45.8	54.4
Mali	21.6	8.6	30.2
Niger	9.6	2.4	12.0
Senegal	20.4	48.5	68.9
Sudan	2.9	40.2	43.1
Tanzania	24.2	31.0	55.2
Togo	40.4	51.6	92.0
Average	18.0	22.5	40.5

Source: Based on Mingat and Tan (1985a).

sion in the primary school budget would be substantial, ranging from 40 to 90 percent. Since Tanzania and Togo have attained or are close to attaining universal primary education, the generated resources could be used to improve educational quality. In the remaining countries, if the additional resources were used for quantitative expansion, the enrollment ratio in primary education would rise dramatically. Given present unit costs, this ratio would increase from 76 to 100 percent in Côte d'Ivoire, 48 to 81 percent in Senegal, and 51 to 73 percent in Sudan (Mingat and Tan 1985a).

In countries with a very low primary school enrollment rate, the returns to primary school expansion are likely to exceed the returns to secondary education and to almost all subjects in higher education. But as coverage at the primary level is extended geographically and academically to a diverse population, the average costs will tend to rise and the marginal returns to fall. In some countries, such as those that are close to attaining universal primary education, it may be socially profitable to use the extra funds to expand secondary education. In countries where highly skilled personnel is relatively scarce, it may be profitable to expand fields within higher education that exhibit high social rates of return, such as engineering, management, or the physical sciences (see appendix table D-3).

Table 7-6. Impact of a 10 Percent Increase in Fees on Enrollment in Public Higher Education if Fee Revenues Were Used to Expand Higher Education

Country	Unit fee as percentage of unit cost	Percentage increase in enrollment if cost elasticity were 0	Percentage increase in enrollment if cost elasticity were −0.5
Africa			
Burundi	14.8	1.7	4.2
Lesotho	5.0	0.5	1.1
Malawi	1.0	0.1	0.2
Nigeria	12.4	1.4	3.3
Asia			
India	29.1	4.1	13.9
Indonesia	13.0	1.5	3.5
Korea, Rep. of	23.4	3.1	8.8
Malaysia	5.8	0.6	1.3
Pakistan	2.1	0.2	0.4
Philippines	3.7	0.4	0.8
Thailand	6.9	0.7	1.6
Turkey	15.0	1.8	4.3
Latin America			
Bolivia	1.0	0.1	0.2
Brazil	5.0	0.5	1.1
Chile	25.0	3.3	10.0
Colombia	3.4	0.4	0.7
Costa Rica	8.0	0.9	1.9
Dominican Rep.	1.0	0.1	0.2
Ecuador	2.0	0.2	0.4
Guatemala	10.0	1.1	2.5
Honduras	10.0	1.1	2.5
Paraguay	0.7	0.1	0.1
Uruguay	5.0	0.5	1.1
Average	8.8	1.1	2.8

Note: Excess demand for higher education is assumed.
Source: Calculated from appendix table D-1, using equation C-18 in appendix C.

The extent to which the higher educational system can expand depends upon the impact of school size on unit costs. The extent to which fee increases can provide additional services depends upon the behavior of unit costs and the presence of scale economies. Since there is little information about the behavior of unit costs, only hypothetical cases based on reasonable assumptions about the unit cost elasticities at the margin are discussed here.

Table 7-6 shows how a 10 percent increase in fees might affect the quantity of public higher education if the revenues were used to expand higher education. On the assumption of constant costs (given that unit fees are, on average, 8.8 percent of unit costs for the sample of countries), this fee increase would result in an increase in enrollment of 1 percent. For countries with a less than average cost-recovery percentage, such as Bolivia, the Dominican Republic, or Malawi (at 1 percent), the increase in enrollment would be 0.1 percent. For countries such as Korea, with a cost-recovery percentage of 23, or Chile, with a cost-recovery percentage of 25, the potential increase in enrollment that could be financed by a 10 percent increase in fees would exceed 3 percent.

On the assumption that there are scale economies in the provision of higher education, the expansionary impact would be enhanced. If average costs declined by 0.5 percent for every 1 percent increase in enrollment (that is, a cost elasticity of -0.5), the potential expansionary impact of a 10 percent increase in fees for the average country would almost triple from 1.1 percent to 2.8 percent. Macro-level evidence indicates that such an estimate of unit cost elasticity is plausible (Psacharopoulos 1982).

Secondary Education

There is less empirical evidence of excess demand for secondary education, although it is known to exist in some places. In Malawi, for example, the supply of secondary school places accommodates only one-third of expressed demand (Tan, Lee, and Mingat 1984). In Kenya, there is evidence that many students retake the secondary entrance examination to enhance their chances of admission (Somerset 1974). There are other indications that private demand is strong, particularly in urban areas. Recent restrictions on secondary school budgets in Pakistan have led to an unprecedented growth in private schools during the past five years (Jimenez and Tan 1985). The same is true in Kenya, where the harambee system of locally financed schools has absorbed those unable to enter publicly provided secondary schools (Bertrand and Griffin 1983).

A case study of the potential impact of fees at the secondary level in Malawi is particularly well documented (Mingat and Tan 1985c). Although only 4 percent of the secondary-school-age population attend school, the government has had to restrain increases in public spending in the sector because of adverse economic conditions. The supply of places for secondary education, as a result, has not kept up with demand. In 1982, the total private demand was estimated to be at least 50,000, but only 17,000 individuals could be accommodated.

The cost per student place in Malawian secondary education was K266 (about US$280) a year in 1982. On average, students paid K30 in tuition and K71 in boarding charges. In total, the revenue from tuition and boarding fees recovered about 38 percent of the entire cost of public secondary education. The actual annual cost to the government of enrolling each student was therefore K165 (0.62 × K266). Despite the already substantial level of private costs, an increase in tuition fees is unlikely to result in lower enrollments. It probably would only reduce the extent of excess demand, not the actual overall level of enrollments, if the extra revenue generated was used solely to increase the supply of secondary education places.

If the elasticity of demand were −0.03, excess demand for secondary education would persist as long as the new level of tuition fees remained below K95 (Mingat and Tan 1986c). If fees were raised to this level, the additional revenue would allow secondary education to expand by 11,000 places, an increase of 65 percent over the current provision. The potential expansion would, of course, be smaller if demand were much more elastic than was assumed in this calculation. Even if elasticity was −1.0 instead of −0.5, however, fees as high as K68 would not eliminate excess demand. The revenue generated by raising fees to this level would permit a smaller expansion of 5,100 extra places, an increase of 30 percent over the present supply. These simulations show that increased user charges for secondary education could generate efficiency gains since the additional resources would allow increased investment in a highly profitable activity.

For other countries where precise estimates of excess demand are not available, only calculations at the margin are possible. The results are presented in table 7-7. On average, a 10 percent increase in fees in twenty-seven developing countries would allow an expansion in enrollment of 2.2 percent if unit costs were unchanged. If unit costs dropped at a unit cost elasticity rate of approximately −0.5, a figure derived from a study of Paraguay and Bolivia by Jimenez (1986a), the expansion would be a substantial 11.1 percent.

Primary Education

It has been argued that mobilizing resources through user chargers for higher and perhaps even secondary education would produce efficiency gains

Table 7-7. Impact of a 10 Percent Increase in Fees on Enrollment in Public Secondary Education if Fee Revenues Were Used to Expand Secondary Education

Country	Unit fee as percentage of unit cost	Percentage increase in enrollment if cost elasticity were 0	Percentage increase in enrollment if cost elasticity were −0.5
Africa			
Botswana	2.7	0.3	0.6
Burundi	6.3	0.7	1.4
Central African Rep.	2.7	0.3	0.6
Kenya	43.7	7.8	69.4
Lesotho	42.1	7.3	53.3
Malawi	38.0	6.1	31.7
Nigeria	39.0	6.4	35.5
Sierra Leone	20.3	2.5	6.8
Swaziland	26.3	3.6	11.1
Togo	5.0	0.5	1.1
Uganda	24.3	3.2	9.5
Zambia	11.6	1.3	3.0
Zimbabwe	5.0	0.5	1.1
Asia			
India	18.5	2.3	5.9
Indonesia	9.0	1.0	2.2
Korea, Rep. of	41.2	7.0	46.8
Malaysia	5.0	0.5	1.1
Pakistan	1.8	0.2	0.4
Solomon Islands	25.0	3.3	10.0
Thailand	12.5	1.4	3.3
Latin America			
Bolivia	0.4	0.0	0.1
Chile	0.9	0.1	0.2
Costa Rica	0.5	0.1	0.1
Haiti	3.4	0.4	0.7
Honduras	9.6	1.1	2.4
Paraguay	2.0	0.2	0.4
Uruguay	0.4	0.0	0.1
Average	14.7	2.2	11.1

Source: Calculated from appendix table D-1, using equation C-18 in appendix C.

if the resources were used to expand the educational service with the highest rate of return. But for the primary level, other factors must be considered, and the conclusion may differ. First, because of externalities and other public goods characteristics, higher unit subsidies are needed to stimulate private demand at the primary level than at other levels. Second, in many countries, there is not as much evidence of excess demand for primary education. There may be some excess demand in urban areas, and, if so, the analysis for higher and secondary education would hold. In rural areas, low enrollment ratios are due as much to lack of demand as to supply constraints. Thus, existing schools may not be able to generate resources without lowering enrollment.

Under certain circumstances, however, it would also be efficient to charge higher prices at the primary level. If transfers of funds from other levels of education are administratively or politically too costly to implement or if these transfers do not generate sufficient resources (as in countries with relatively small enrollments at tertiary levels), then resources could be generated through higher user charges for primary education.

If there is excess demand at the primary level, then the previous analysis holds. If not, the argument hinges on the demand for the quality of education. It is assumed that the lack of private demand for existing school places is due predominantly to the poor quality of the schooling. Thus, if parents and students knew that the additional resources would be used to improve school quality, they would be willing to pay the higher user charges. The structure of demand would then change. In fact, demand would increase as a result of the fee increase, if the fees were used to improve schools.

One indication that primary school quality is low in developing countries is the shortage of textbooks and other school supplies. In Burkina Faso, for example, where books are provided free by the state at the primary level, "probably only a minority of pupils possess textbooks" (Orivel 1983, 12). In rural Mali, there are about six textbooks per one hundred primary students, and seven out of twenty schools surveyed had no books at all (Birdsall 1983a, 10). In Kenya, despite an education commission's recommendation in 1976 that government expenditure on supplies and equipment be doubled, such resources appear to be declining (Bertrand and Griffin 1983, 34). Other indications of low quality include severe overcrowding and relatively high student-teacher ratios, such as in Malawi (Thobani 1983, 26), and a great reliance on untrained primary teachers (Bertrand and Griffin 1983, 32).

Partly because of the difficulty in agreeing upon an appropriate definition of educational quality, direct evidence on the social returns to investment in quality is not extensive. The preceding evidence suggests, however, that the mix of quantity and quality in primary education may be inappropriate. Behrman and Birdsall (1983) conclude that the high social rate of return to primary schooling in Brazil can be largely ascribed to quality-enhancing rather than quantity-enhancing investments. The relative neglect of quality is partly explained by the recurrent cost problem outlined earlier. Moreover, most internationally set standards regarding schooling are based solely on quantity (such as universal education to a certain level). Providers who are intent on meeting those standards with a given amount of resources may sacrifice quality to expand coverage. Ignoring the tradeoff between numbers and quality of learning is likely to result in a misallocation of resources.

The imposition of user charges on quantity (the charge is levied per child) may induce a more efficient mix by decreasing utilization and allowing revenues to be used to increase quality. This is feasible because improved quality may stimulate demand and increase households' willingness to pay (Birdsall 1983b). Thus, any fees collected to expand quality may also allow society to expand coverage (financed by user fees), that is, to increase the number of primary students who are educated. Since fees are often earmarked for books and supplies, modest increases in fees may have a small impact on the total government recurrent budget but a substantial effect on certain types of expenditures. For example, Birdsall (1983a) estimates that in Mali a 10 percent increase in user fees would be sufficient to double the supply of books available to students. Since the availability of books, in particular, and school quality, in general, affect learning throughout the world (see Heyneman and Loxley 1983), this would seem to be a great contribution not only to finance, but also to internal efficiency. The social gains depend upon the benefits of another unit of quality in relation to quantity.

Birdsall's (1983a) model of this argument is depicted in figure 7-1, where the q axis denotes the quantity of education being provided, given the quality. Initially, no prices are charged, and for a school of a given quality, provided at the cost to the government c_p c_0, the private demand structure is D_p^0. There is no willingness to pay for schooling. If c_p denotes the private cost of providing education, demand will be q_0. If the government provides a subsidy of S_0, this demand will be met. S_0 is the iso-subsidy line (see explanation of figure 6-1). At a higher quality level, it would be more costly to provide education, at c_1. But there would be greater willingness to pay, as well, at D_p^1. If the subsidy allocation remained the same at S_0, prices could be raised from zero to $p_1 c_p$ and enrollment could still expand to q_1. Because little is known about key behavioral parameters, such as the responsiveness of demand to changes in quality, the relative preference for quantity over quality, and the costs of increasing quality, this model has yet to be tested. Some of the conceptual and empirical work, however, has begun (Mingat and Tan 1986b).

If there is no excess demand for primary education, the effect of a fee increase would depend upon the elasticity of demand. Consider, for example, the potential role of user charges in primary education as a response to a cut in government subsidies. The revenue from user charges could be used to

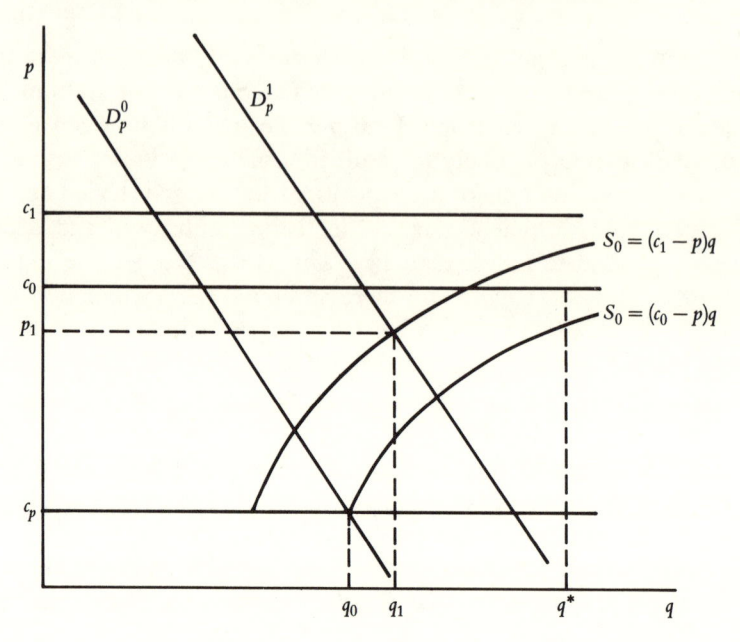

Figure 7-1. Enrollment Expansion as the Result of Increased Fees to Finance Qualitative Improvements

minimize the contractionary impact of tighter budgetary restrictions.

Figure 7-2 presents the financial impact of a marginal (10 percent) cut in government transfers to primary education and the increase in fee that would be necessary to maintain present enrollments. It is assumed that, at the current fee level, the system is at equilibrium with neither excess demand nor excess supply. A drop in the subsidy allocation from S_0 to S_1 would result in a drop in enrollment from q_0 to q_1. To mitigate this drop would require a price increase from zero to $c_p p_2$. The welfare gain obtained would be $ABED$.

The results of the analysis are presented in table 7-8. For the countries for which data are available, a drop of 10 percent in government subsidies would require a price increase of 9.4 percent to minimize social losses if demand is relatively inelastic, or 5.3 percent if demand is unit elastic.

Prices and Efficiency within Schools

Two common sources of internal inefficiency are the mix of purchased inputs, such as teachers' services and pedagogical materials, and the process of selecting students.

Figure 7-2. Impact of a Cut in Subsidies on Fees and Enrollment in Public Primary Education

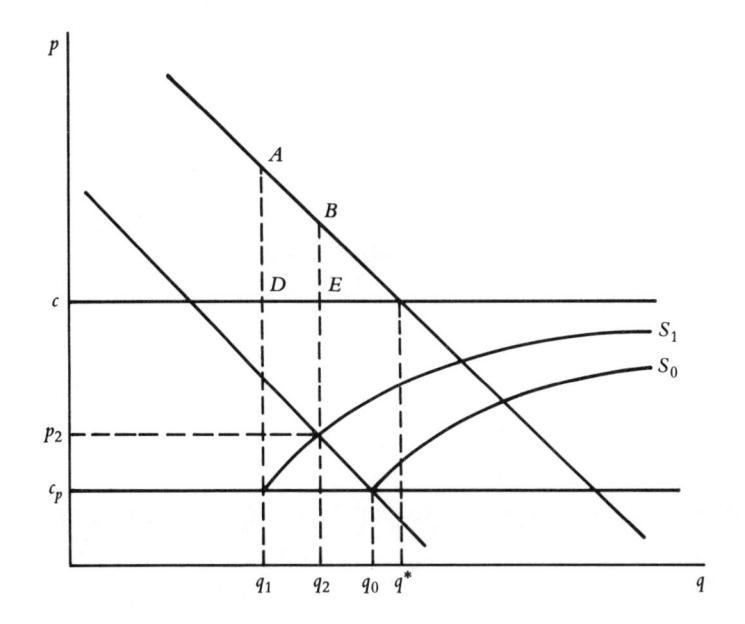

Buying the Right Inputs

The mix of inputs is inefficient when more can be achieved if the same amount of funds is allocated differently among the various inputs. The present financing and provision of education contributes to this type of inefficiency. Most public school systems are highly centralized, both in the collection and distribution of revenue for education. Revenues are usually drawn from general tax sources, which are then distributed through budgetary allocations to the central ministry of education. In turn, the funds are allocated to schools and universities according to preset funding formulas. In many instances the central budgets pay teachers directly.

In most cases the public school system has adjusted to new budgetary restrictions through a process of default, partly because managers have neither the incentive nor the authority to respond creatively. Rules regarding teachers' qualifications, employment, and salaries are normally inflexible, largely because teacher unions are a powerful force in defining and protecting the status quo. In most cases teachers are employed centrally, and individual schools have no discretion over hiring. Consequently, much of the reduction in education funds has been absorbed by cuts in expenditure for

Table 7-8. **Impact of a 10 Percent Cut in Subsidies on Fees and Enrollment in Public Primary Education if Household Payments Were Used to Maintain Equilibrium**

	Unit fee as percentage of unit cost	Percentage increase in fee if demand elasticity were		Percentage decrease in enrollment if fees rise and demand elasticity were	
Country		−0.5	−1.0	−0.5	−1.0
Africa					
Botswana	0.0	20.0	10.0	−10.0	−10.0
Burkina Faso	13.0	0.7	0.7	−0.4	−0.7
Burundi	0.0	20.0	10.0	−10.0	−10.0
Central African Rep.	2.5	3.3	2.9	−1.7	−2.9
Guinea	0.0	20.0	10.0	−10.0	−10.0
Kenya	4.0	2.2	2.0	−1.1	−2.0
Lesotho	9.0	1.1	1.0	−0.5	−1.0
Malawi	37.0	0.3	0.3	−0.1	−0.3
Mauritania	0.0	20.0	10.0	−10.0	−10.0
Nigeria	30.0	0.3	0.3	−0.2	−0.3
Sierra Leone	1.5	5.0	4.0	−2.5	−4.0
Swaziland	7.0	1.3	1.3	−0.7	−1.3
Togo	13.0	0.7	0.7	−0.4	−0.7
Uganda	27.0	0.4	0.4	−0.2	−0.4
Zambia	3.0	2.9	2.5	−0.4	−2.5
Zimbabwe	0.0	20.0	10.0	−10.0	−10.0
Asia					
India	2.0	4.0	3.3	−2.0	−3.3
Indonesia	0.0	20.0	10.0	−10.0	−10.0
Korea, Rep. of	3.7	2.4	2.1	−1.2	−2.1
Malaysia	5.0	1.8	1.7	−0.9	−1.7
Pakistan	1.2	5.9	4.5	−2.9	−4.5
Solomon Islands	0.0	20.0	10.0	−10.0	−10.0
Thailand	0.0	20.0	10.0	−10.0	−10.0
Turkey	0.0	20.0	10.0	−10.0	−10.0
Latin America					
Bolivia	0.8	7.7	5.6	−3.8	−5.6
Chile	1.6	4.8	3.8	−2.4	−3.8
Costa Rica	0.3	12.5	7.7	−6.3	−7.7
Dominican Rep.	0.0	20.0	10.0	−10.0	−10.0
Ecuador	0.0	20.0	10.0	−10.0	−10.0
Haiti	6.8	1.4	1.3	−0.7	−1.3
Honduras	0.0	20.0	10.0	−10.0	−10.0
Paraguay	4.1	2.2	2.0	−1.1	−2.0
Uruguay	0.5	10.0	6.7	−5.0	−6.7
Average	5.2	9.4	5.3	−4.7	−5.3

Source: Calculated from appendix table D-1, using equation C-11 in appendix C.

other categories of school inputs. For example, in East African countries, such as Comoros, Ethiopia, Rwanda, and Tanzania, governments are currently facing difficulties in maintaining textbook programs. The result is severe textbook shortages, especially in rural areas (Wolff 1984). Similarly, in Jamaica there is a general lack of instructional materials in primary schools and in some secondary schools, despite the fact that 20 percent of the state budget is allocated to the education sector. In fact, in most developing countries today expenditure on instructional materials is very low (1980 US$4.80 on average; for developed countries, the figure is 1980 US$106). On average in 1980, it accounts for 3.4 percent of the total public recurrent expenditure on education (Unesco, *Statistical Yearbook*). Examples from Heller and Cheasty (1984) in Latin America have already been mentioned.

A financing system that relied more heavily on user charges could improve efficiency since it would give schools more resources with which to respond to local conditions. The willingness to pay of households could be mobilized to buy the necessary inputs. School authorities would have to be held accountable to parents and students to ensure that appropriate incentives existed for management.

Choosing the Right Students

A system of selecting students is likely to be inefficient if it does not admit from the previous level the students with the most learning potential. If it is assumed that innate ability is randomly distributed in the population, then a system that grants access solely on the basis of willingness to pay would lead to inefficient selection.

Even with free or heavily subsidized education, poor bright students are being left out. In Colombia, 54 percent of first-year students in higher education institutions scored lower on aptitude tests than did the corresponding cohort of secondary school graduates who did not continue their education. The students who did not continue their education came from families with incomes significantly lower than those of the families whose children enrolled in institutions of higher education (Jimenez 1985).

Since there is a lack of credit markets from which students can borrow to finance their studies, the competition for places is limited to those who have the requisite private funds at the time of enrollment. Greater reliance on user fees might exacerbate this type of inefficiency because it would force some of the poorer students to terminate their education. The extent to which the users would be affected depends, of course, on the magnitude of the price increase. Tables 7-9 to 7-11 show the distributional impact on household budgets caused by a price change that would recover all costs. Since there is

Table 7-9. Household Expenditure for Public Education without Subsidies in Malaysia

(1974 ringgit; all items per household)

Quintile	Average annual income (Y)	Current public subsidy	Total public cost Amount	Total public cost Percentage of Y	Out-of-pocket cost Amount	Out-of-pocket cost Percentage of Y
1	1,552	471	583	38	221	18
2	2,681	419	527	20	215	10
3	3,786	483	585	15	295	10
4	5,230	419	511	9	288	8
5	12,440	422	513	4	291	6
Mean	5,662	444	544	13	265	10

Source: Meerman (1979), tables 3.1, 4.7, and 4.14.

Table 7-10. Household Expenditure for Public Education without Subsidies in Colombia

(1974 Colombian pesos; all items per household)

Quintile	Average annual income (Y)	Primary Amount	Primary Percentage of Y	Secondary Amount	Secondary Percentage of Y	University Amount	University Percentage of Y	Total Amount	Total Percentage of Y
1	10,368	1,305	12.6	598	5.8	18	—	1,921	18.4
2	17,820	1,089	6.1	776	4.4	96	0.5	1,961	11.0
3	25,032	835	3.3	751	3.0	224	0.9	1,810	7.2
4	36,912	589	1.6	872	2.4	489	1.3	1,950	5.3
5	104,388	252	0.2	555	0.5	1,257	1.2	2,064	1.9
Mean	38,904	816	2.1	718	1.8	413	1.1	1,947	5.0

Source: Selowsky (1979), tables 3.14 and 3.15.

no information about the precise market characteristics or price and income elasticities for Malaysia, Colombia, and Indonesia, the calculations in the tables are made on the assumption of no change in utilization and constant unit costs. The impact on out-of-pocket costs borne by users is evident, for example, in the Malaysian figures. If the educational subsidies ended, the average household would have to devote only 13 percent of its income to finance all the public costs of education services, but its out-of-pocket costs

Table 7-11. **Household Expenditure for Public Education without Subsidies in Indonesia**
(1980 rupiah; all items per household)

Income group	Average annual income (Y)	Public cost (primary and secondary) Amount	Public cost (primary and secondary) Percentage of Y	Educational expenditure as percentage of Y
Lowest 40 percent	173,016	62,168	35.9	1.19
Middle 30 percent	297,792	64,952	21.8	1.60
Highest 30 percent	717,060	72,839	10.2	2.26
Mean	353,820	65,879	18.6	1.86

Note: Household income is approximated by household expenditure.
Source: Indonesia Census Bureau (SUSENAS), 1983 data.

would rise to 23 percent. Lower-income households would probably find financing the full costs of education excessive, even if out-of-pocket costs were disregarded. Similar findings hold for Indonesia. If all households were made to pay the full social cost of education, at present levels of enrollment, the proportion of household expenditure devoted to education would rise from 2 percent to 19 percent. For the poorest 40 percent of the income distribution, it would rise to 36 percent.

To mitigate any potentially harmful effects from this type of inefficiency, two policy measures should accompany increased user charges: continued subsidization of education, but with the subsidies targeted at low-income groups (by testing both merit and means, or ability to pay) to ensure that they are appropriately represented in the pool of applicants; and student loans to ease the capital market constraint, particularly at higher levels of education.

Scholarships. Merit- and means-tested scholarships account for only a small part of the total subsidies distributed by governments. As documented earlier, most subsidies are distributed evenly across the board, usually in the form of almost nonexistent tuition but in some cases as direct payments to all successful applicants.

An argument was made earlier to use revenues from a fee increase to expand the provision of school places. If this policy were combined with a rise in means-tested scholarships, the expansionary impact would be somewhat reduced. The net effect, however, could still be beneficial. For Malawian secondary schools, if the fee elasticity of demand were -0.5 and if fees were raised from K30 to K95, 43.9 percent of the currently enrolled students would drop out. To neutralize this adverse effect on equity, it would be necessary to shield these students from the fee increase. Suppose that they were fully compensated through scholarships equal to the amount of the fee increase. (This is a conservative assumption since some of the dropouts might be able to continue their studies with smaller scholarships.) Under this scheme, the increase in fees from K30 to K95 would permit secondary education in Malawi to expand from the present provision of 17,000 places to 23,200 places, whereas in the absence of scholarships 28,100 places could be provided. (See Mingat and Tan 1986c for a fuller discussion.)

Student Loans. One way of minimizing the negative equity and efficiency effects of increasing private financing is to improve individuals' access to financial markets through student loan schemes, particularly for higher education.

In some countries, commercial credit markets work well but may not be available for funding education or training. Private banks may be unwilling to lend to students because they often lack acceptable forms of collateral. Also, banks may be afraid that unemployment will cause graduates to default on their loans. And in many developing countries, the legal and administrative frameworks for enforcing financing contracts are weak. Finally, the administrative costs of collection tend to be high because of the mobility of graduates. Many commercial banks in developing countries are simply too small to absorb the high risks and costs of lending to students without charging prohibitive interest rates.

Governments can make it easier for students to obtain educational credit. Because their size allows them to absorb the risks that private lenders are unwilling or unable to bear, governments can become lenders, or they can insure commercial loans. In addition, governments can make collections less problematic. Since most graduates work in the formal wage sector, they can be traced through the government bureaucracy or through the income tax system. With governmental authority, employers may be willing to assist collection by making deductions from wages for loan repayment.

In several developed and developing countries, particularly in Latin America, the government is already active in providing educational credit (see table 7-12). Governments either have established state-owned banks to provide student loans, particularly for higher education, or have encouraged private banks to provide student loans with a government guarantee. The Colombian government has recently introduced a type of loan that is repaid partly by the students and partly by their parents. This is similar to the PLUS scheme (Parents' Loans for Undergraduate Study) in the United States that permits parents and students to borrow from the government to finance education.

Table 7-12. **Student Loans in Latin America, 1978**

Country (student loan institution)	Total loans awarded (excluding loans already repaid)
Argentina (INCE)	1,400
Bolivia (CIDEP)	476
Brazil	
APLUB	3,084
Caixa Economica Federal	354,588
Colombia (ICETEX)	53,865
Costa Rica (CONAPE)	1,286
Chile (Catholic University)	1,982
Dominican Republic (FCE)	10,097
Ecuador (IECE)	15,803
El Salvador (Educredito)	2,350
Honduras (Educredito)	1,740
Jamaica (Students' Loan Bureau)	6,875
Nicaragua (Educredito)	630
Panama (IFARHU)	5,800
Peru (INABEC)	274
Venezuela	
Educredito	2,866
SACUEDO	2,770

Source: Woodhall (1983).

Experience with student loan programs shows that high default rates and collection difficulties are sometimes exaggerated. In the United States, default rates on student loans have been falling in recent years. When allowance is made for funds collected on previously defaulted loans, the net annual default rate in 1981 was only 4 percent, which compares well with the default rate on other forms of credit (Hauptman 1983). In the developing countries, it is more difficult to evaluate the incidence of default since loan schemes are relatively recent and a high proportion of loans are not yet due. Latin America and parts of the Caribbean are probably the only developing regions with extensive experience with loan schemes. The incidence of default or late repayment has actually been quite low in several of these countries. In Costa Rica, only 0.5 percent of the debts due for repayment in 1978 were in default. In Brazil, the proportion was only 2 percent, and in Colombia, Honduras, Jamaica, and Mexico, it was between 5 and 11 percent (Woodhall 1983).

Evidence from a few countries suggests that administrative costs are not exorbitantly high. In Sweden, the Central Student Assistance Commitee, the state agency responsible for administering student loans and other forms of assistance, calculated that in 1980–81 the cost of administration represented only 1.8 percent of its total expenditure on student aid. And the U.S. Congressional Budget Office estimated in 1980 that the annual cost of servicing student loans in the United States ranged from 1.5 to 2 percent of the loan principal, compared with the usual range of 0.25 to 3.75 percent with housing loans (Woodhall 1983). In several Latin American student loan institutions, from 12 to 23 percent of the total annual outlay was spent on administration. With good management, however, it would be possible to reduce this share to between 10 and 15 percent (Herrick, Shavlach, and Seville 1974).

Although loan schemes tend to suffer from default and collection problems, these difficulties are neither unmanageable nor universal. The cost of administration can be kept reasonably low in most cases. In the absence of well-functioning commercial credit markets, individuals often must rely on funds borrowed from relatives, friends, or ad hoc moneylenders. In Malawi, more than half of the secondary school students in high and low socioeconomic groups obtained financing from relatives in 1983 and another 20 percent obtained external loans (Tan, Lee, and Mingat 1984, table 4). Not all students, however, know people who are willing and able to lend them money.

A Further Efficiency Gain: Overcoming Rent Seeking. Quantity rationing schemes, such as entrance examinations or grades, may still rely on willingness to pay. Many relatively wealthy students invest in private tutoring or repeat grades to improve their examination scores and thereby improve their chances of gaining access to the next level of education. This "overeducation" is unproductive and consumes resources.

High education subsidies are a windfall to those who are able to obtain them. They impart economic rents; that is, they offer a private benefit that exceeds the social cost of provision. This gives an incentive for those with means to invest resources in order to receive the subsidies. In economic terms, this is called rent seeking. Thus, students may deliberately repeat grades so as to compete more successfully for subsidies at higher levels of education, as in Malawi, and schools may overexpand or lobby the ministry of education, depending upon the rules regarding the provision of subsidies. Private providers can also engage in renk seeking if subsidies are distributed to them. In Kenya, many harambee schools are being established without much regard for financial viability because they expect to be subsidized in the future (Bertrand and Griffin 1983).

Prices and Equity

To a large extent, inequities in the access to education would be alleviated by user charges that are accompanied by student loans and subsidies targeted to low-income groups. Moreover, the shift in subsidies from higher to primary education would, in itself, improve equity (Mingat and Tan 1985a).

In developing countries as a group, 72 percent of a generation of schoolchildren (those with primary schooling or less) obtain only 25 percent of the total public expenditure on education (Mingat and Tan 1985a). Their share would increase to 64 percent if user charges could be introduced to recover all the costs of higher education and if the public resources that were generated could be used to finance additional primary school places for those who are currently denied access.

The redirection of subsidies toward primary education would also benefit those from low-income groups. At present, such groups receive very little of the education subsidies, whereas the high-income groups receive the most. In Chile, Colombia, Indonesia, and Malaysia, students from low-income families receive between 6 percent and 10 percent of the subsidies at the university level, whereas those in the high-income group receive between 50 percent and 83 percent (see table 7-13). This is because the low-income groups are grossly underrepresented at this level of education. This inequitable outcome would be redressed by increasing subsidization at the primary level, where the low-income groups are most widely represented.

As noted earlier in the discussion of student selection, any adverse equity effect within higher education might be neutralized through selective scholarships or exempting low-income students from paying fees. In some Latin American countries, university fees are related to family income;

Table 7-13. The Share of Higher Education Subsidies by Income Group

| | Income group | | |
Country	Low[a]	Middle	High
Chile	6	44	50
Colombia	6	35	60
Indonesia	7	10	83
Malaysia	10	38	51

a. The low-income group corresponds to the poorest 40 percent, except in the case of Chile, where it corresponds to the poorest 30 percent.
Source: Appendix table D-4.

students from poor families pay lower tuition fees than those from wealthier ones. A means-tested scholarship system would achieve the same result.

Private Schools

Another way to shift the financing burden to users is to allow private schools to provide more education. In some countries, however, private schools and universities are not allowed to operate. For example, the People's Republic of the Congo, Ethiopia, and, more recently, Nigeria have abolished or have attempted to ban private schools through legislative action (Cowen and McLean 1984). Lifting such a ban would lead to an expansion in education, as in Pakistan, where the nationalization policy of the 1970s has recently been reversed.

A more widely practiced form of restriction is the imposition of a set of norms regarding fees, the hiring of teachers, their qualifications and pay, curriculum development, and student selection. Although ostensibly less binding than outright prohibition, such regulations may have a stifling effect on private schools. The extent to which private education is discouraged depends upon the degree of regulation. In Cameroon, for example, the government determines the fee charged by private schools; similarly, in Colombia and Chile, private school fees are controlled by the government (Schiefelbein 1985). Other countries, such as Jordan and Zambia, have simply declared that all primary education must be free. Relaxing overly restrictive regulation, while monitoring to ensure against fraudulent institutions, would lead to educational expansion.

This is not a recommendation for a completely private system, which would tend to provide less education than would be optimal. When public budgets are constrained, however, the coexistence of private and public systems would allow more flexibility in expanding educational resources, especially if there are constraints on raising fees for public schools.

Figure 7-3 depicts the social gain from loosening restrictions in the private sector. The private and social demand curves are, respectively, D_p and D_s. To simplify the presentation, private nonfee costs are not shown in the diagram. Suppose that the long-run marginal cost of private and public schools is the same for both types of schools and constant at c. The effective supply curve for an underfunded public school system would be given by the iso-subsidy line S. If there was a cap on user charges that the public system could levy at $\hat{p}$, only q_0 students could be accommodated at a certain quality level. With a restriction on private schools, this would lead to an effective excess demand of $q_0 q_1$. But if the restrictions were lifted, the private sector would offer school places to cover costs. Initially, the first private school owners would be

Figure 7-3. The Social Gain from Loosening Restrictions in the Private Sector

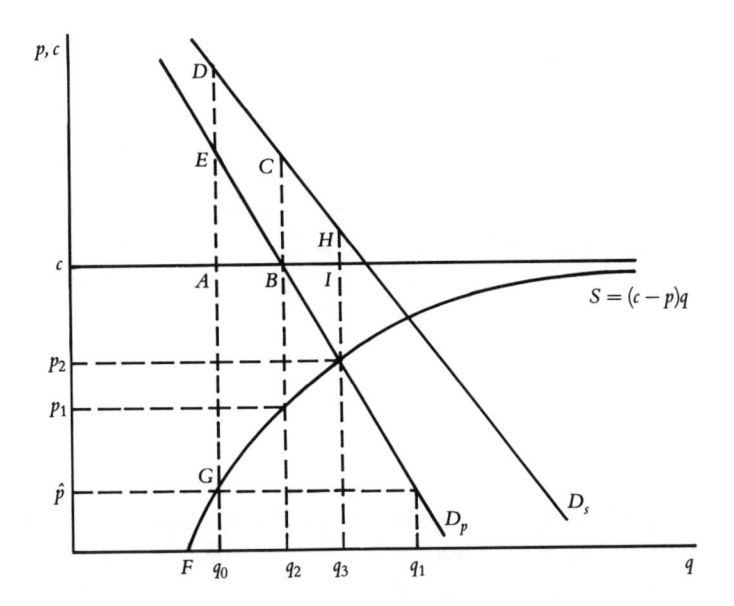

able to charge a price Eq_0 and might earn "economic profit"—profits in excess of a competitively determined rate of return. With free entry, however, prices would be bid down to c, where proprietors would recover a reasonable return on their investment. Economic profits would eventually drop to nil. The "effective" supply curve in this mixed system would be line segment FG for quantities provided less than q_0, and the straight line denoted by AI for quantities provided greater than q_0. The social gain from allowing the private sector to operate is $DCBA$.

Notice the following:

- An increase in prices of public schools from $\hat{p}$ to p_1 would have the same social benefit as a policy of easing the restriction on private schools. The difference would be in the distribution of the benefits. The amount ABq_2q_0 accrues to the owners of schools rather than to the government or to parents and students in the latter policy.
- This policy of allowing a mixed public-private system is dominated by one which raises prices in the public system until effective excess demand is eliminated. A price increase in the public system to p_2 would result in an additional gain of $CHIB$ relative to free entry in the private market. The reason is that the externalities to schooling are not taken into account by the private system.

Greater reliance on private provision could have negative efficiency and equity effects in terms of access. This can be mitigated to some extent by introducing a more selective entrance procedure in public institutions so that the meritorious needy are given priority. But to avoid a segregated system in which the poor go to public schools (which may be of high quality) and the rich to private schools, subsidies could be distributed to students for use in private schools.

Governments subsidize private schools in many developing countries. The subsidized provider is not necessarily less efficient than one that is not subsidized. It is the disposition of the proceeds that is important in determining efficiency. A sector that does not provide incentives for its owners and managers to minimize costs will be less efficient than another that does. A private system has such incentives imbedded in its structure because the returns flow to the owners, who can keep or sell their shares. A public system may not have such incentives since the owners—the general public—cannot transfer their shares in the enterprise and capitalize on any of the gains. Thus, subsidies to a private school system may still result in cost minimization.

Education subsidies are, for the most part, uniformly distributed to all enrolled students because the school is usually the recipient. An alternative is for the government to channel the subsidy to the student rather than to the institution. For example, recipients of grants or scholarships would be chosen according to their academic performance and economic need and permitted to attend the schools of their choice, whether public or private. This arrangement would broaden parental and student choices, increase institutional accountability, and encourage schools to compete for pupils, thus stimulating diversity and experimentation and improving efficiency.

The option of distributing centrally collected subsidies to individual students directly may be particularly beneficial at the levels of higher and even secondary education, where students and their families are likely to have more information about educational alternatives. At lower levels, the administrative costs of distributing scholarships and providing information about schools may be high enough to preclude the possibility of individual distribution of subsidies. An alternative might be to distribute subsidies to local authorities or neighborhood groups according to the economic needs of the groups. For example, communities in rural areas would be provided relatively more subsidies than would neighborhoods in urban areas. Local authorities could then use the centrally provided subsidies, local levies (both monetary and nonmonetary), and user fees to purchase the educational services desired by their constituents. The central government's subsidy formula could be structured to encourage local authorities to be more fiscally independent. The local group could be rewarded, for example, by a matching grant, in which case subsidies would be partly based on locally raised funds.

Public subsidization of private education is not widespread. In developing countries, individually distributed public subsidies for private education are limited. In Pakistan, for example, the government has recently announced plans to establish scholarship programs at all levels of education for the children of families with limited income, but it did not specify the extent to which scholarship recipients would be allowed to attend private schools. In some Latin American countries, between 5 and 10 percent of the private secondary students receive scholarships provided by their school, usually in the form of exemptions from fees (Schiefelbein 1985). In other countries, such as Colombia, the government exerts pressure on private schools to provide education to poor students by requiring the schools to increase their scholarships in exchange for official permission to raise fees.

Governments can also indirectly subsidize private schools by giving income tax relief on private educational expenditures. In Brazil, for example, tax exemptions for families paying private school fees were equivalent in 1972 to 3 percent of total public educational expenditures (Brodersohn and Sanjuro 1978). The feasibility of Brazil's system for other countries depends on their methods of tax collection.

8

Changing Pricing Policy in Health

THE EFFICIENCY AND EQUITY gains from increasing the role of pricing in the provision and allocation of health services, as in the case of education, vary with the type of service. The important criteria for determining this role are the service's public goods characteristics and initial market conditions, the responsiveness of demand and supply to price changes, and the administrative costs of implementing a pricing and collection scheme.

Because it is so varied, health care is generally more difficult to categorize in terms of these criteria than is education. It encompasses individual health care, disease control, and drug provision, as well as programs indirectly related to health such as water supply, sanitation, education, the environment, and housing. Health care can be provided by delivery systems that range from rural clinics to modern hospitals administered by local, regional, or national authorities. (See appendix table D-5 for an example of these health care services and their providers.) Although the mix varies from country to country, a useful categorization scheme shown in table 8-1 has been devised by de Ferranti (1985).

Curative health care includes "first-contact" services, mostly for outpatients. The benefits from using these services tend to accrue almost exclusively to individuals. Thus, there is no case for externalities. Moreover, users have adequate knowledge of these benefits. They do not generally need to know more than they learn from personal experience. Guided by the degree of pain or other symptoms, most individuals know when they are ill or injured and when they should seek medical help.

Another type of curative health care is "referred," and it usually involves the use of inpatient hospital services. Referral services have two types of public goods characteristics. First, the consumer has less knowledge of what is needed to cure a malady, and thus, in a pay-for-service scheme, suppliers may have the incentive to offer more services than would be warranted. Second, for serious cases the cure, such as a prolonged hospital stay, may be unaffordable if patients are not adequately covered by health insurance.

Table 8-1. **Stylized Market Characteristics of Different Types of Health Services**

Type of service	"Public good" characteristic	Market characteristic
Curative care (includes patient care by health facilities and independent providers and purchases by users of medicines) "First-contact" services (mostly outpatient) Referral services (inpatient and some outpatient)	Lack of access to insurance market (inpatient case); lack of knowledge (referral services)	Excess demand in some countries
Preventive care: patient-related (includes well baby and child health care, such as immunization, growth monitoring, and child-care instruction)	Externalities (immunization, perinatal care to avoid permanent disability); lack of knowledge of benefits	No excess demand
Preventive care: non-patient-related (includes disease control, sanitation, promotion of health and hygiene, control of pests and zoonotic disease, and monitoring of disease patterns)	Exclusivity; externalities; lack of knowledge of benefits	Cannot be determined

Source: Adapted from de Ferranti (1985), p. 67.

Some patient-related preventive services, such as immunization, also benefit nonusers. Because these services hinder the spread of disease to other people, externalities are an important consideration in pricing policy. Externalities may also play a role in perinatal and infant care because without this care the chances of long-term disability may be large, and this may affect the welfare of others. For example, if medical services are subsidized, others will have to bear the possible cost of childhood infirmities because of lack of infant care.

Non-patient-related preventive care has almost all the characteristics of a public good, including nonexclusivity. These characteristics imply that a greater role for pricing policy is infeasible for non-patient-related preventive care, which accounts for roughly 3 to 10 percent of all health expenditures in developing countries. Although increased prices are feasible for patient-related preventive care, which accounts for 10 to 20 percent of total health expenditures, the extent of the efficient increase would be constrained if externalities were large. For curative health care, which represents 70 to 87 percent of total health care, increased user charges can be feasible and efficient in the allocation and provision of health services (de Ferranti 1983).

This chapter, an application and extension of the earlier analysis of education pricing, will discuss how increasing user charges for curative health care influences efficiency and equity. The evidence is not based on ex post evaluation of price increases but on simulations of possible effects. Estimated behavioral models are used.

Behavioral Parameters

Before the possible effects of pricing on the provision and allocation of health services can be determined, it is necessary to consider the impact of pricing on demand and supply.

Demand

To make the best decisions about health care services, policymakers must be able to determine the demand for them. This is very difficult, however, because illnesses occur randomly and in different severities. It is also difficult for policymakers to assess the benefits of health services because placing an explicit value on human life is distasteful. Thus, health care policies are more difficult to analyze than are educational policies because health care information is scarce for developing countries, and the analyst must frequently rely upon indirect evidence. Nonetheless, policymakers can work with several indicators to formulate desirable health care policies. For example, most health care policies tend to affect morbidity rates, which can be measured through productivity rates. A healthy work force produces more than does one in which illness keeps workers at home or in the hospital. Policymakers may also look at consumption levels of health services to assess how people perceive the benefits of seeking health care.

Household decisions about the consumption of curative health services depend upon the random incidence of illness, the cost of the services, and the income, size, and location of the consuming household. Consumption of these services also depends upon how much the household spends on prevention.

The few microeconomic estimates that have been done indicate that health demand, whether measured by expenditure or utilization, is relatively unresponsive to price. Heller (1975) finds that the fee elasticity of outpatient visits

Table 8-2. Income and Price Elasticites of the Demand for Health Care in Developing Countries

Country	Latest year of data	Dependent variable	Income Measure	Income Elasticity	Price Measure	Price Elasticity
El Salvador[a]	1980	Medical expenditure	Monthly income	0.887	Distance	−0.054
Malaysia	ca. 1975					
Private		Outpatient visits	Monthly income	11.32	Private fee	−0.15
					Government fee	−0.01
					Private waiting time	−0.25
					Private travel time	−0.14
					Government travel time	−0.18
Government		Outpatient visits	Monthly income	−11.43	Private fee	0.15
					Government fee	−0.01
					Private waiting time	−0.07
					Government travel time	0.10
					Private travel time	0.26
					Government travel time	−0.05
Mali	1982	Willingness to pay for a health worker	Monthly income	—	Distance to dispensary	−0.0003
					Distance to drug outlet	−0.0001
					Quality of dispensary	−0.18
					Quality of output	0.04

(Table continues on the following page.)

Table 8-2 (continued)

Country	Latest year of data	Dependent variable	Income Measure	Income Elasticity	Price Measure	Price Elasticity
Philippines	ca. 1980	Expenditures on drugs	Monthly income	—	Distance to dispensary	−0.002
					Distance to drug outlet	0.0009
					Quality of dispensary	−0.45
					Quality of outlet	0.17

— Not available.
a. For Santa Ana only.
Sources: World Bank data for El Salvador; Heller (1975) for Malaysia; Birdsall and Chuhan (1983) for Mali; and Akin and others (1982) for Philippines.

is significantly less than unity in Malaysia (see table 8-2). Akin and others (1982) conclude that price has no effect at all on outpatient visits in the Philippines.

Relatively price-inelastic demand for health care is not surprising because health care is often viewed as a necessity. But this is not necessarily true for specific categories of health care (outpatient visits, for example) since substitutes, such as private sector services, may be available. The surprising finding is that the cross-price elasticity of these substitutes is small. One possible explanation for the finding of low elasticity is a measurement problem. Prices may be positively correlated with quality; thus the researcher concerned with measurement will find the dampening effect of prices on demand counterbalanced as health care becomes relatively more expensive. This problem can be resolved only through careful control of quality in future studies.

Finally, elasticity need not be constant. The estimated elasticities are measured in environments where consumers pay very low prices. Price responsiveness may be higher at higher price levels. It is apparent that considerably more research is needed in this area.

Table 8-3 presents only aggregate evidence of the price elasticity of demand for health care. The table shows the demand for personal care, which includes medical expenditures, to be only one component of health care, albeit a major one (Lluch, Powell, and Williams 1977). The time series data for seventeen countries estimate a price elasticity that averages −0.6. For the poorer countries, the price elasticity tends to be somewhat lower—as low as

Table 8-3. Personal Health Care Expenditures

	Average share of budget	Total expenditure elasticity	Price elasticity	Per capita subsistence expenditure[a] (1970 U.S. dollars)
Australia	0.057	2.34	−0.85	14.1
Germany, Fed. Rep.	0.037	1.21	−0.86	6.1
Greece	0.036	1.35	−0.80	3.3
Ireland	0.013	1.07	−0.30	6.3
Israel	0.066	0.99	−0.24	51.6
Italy	0.063	1.04	−0.62	19.8
Jamaica	0.026	2.35	−1.21	−2.4
Korea, Rep. of	0.042	1.76	−0.23	3.7
Panama	0.047	0.92	−0.52	11.2
Philippines	0.035	1.72	−0.22	3.5
Puerto Rico	0.069	1.70	−1.28	−20.6
South Africa	0.048	1.02	−0.20	17.4
Sweden	0.037	1.43	−0.93	3.8
Taiwan	0.057	1.69	−0.46	4.9
Thailand	0.056	0.93	−0.46	3.4
United Kingdom	0.023	1.35	−0.78	6.3
United States	0.081	1.69	−0.92	14.9
Mean Values[b]				
100–500		1.53	0.34	
501–1,000		1.10	−0.51	
1,001–1,500		1.20	−0.61	
1,500+		1.60	0.87	
Overall		1.39	−0.60	

a. The estimated parameters of a Stone-Geary utility function. The numbers are interpreted as the cost of the minimum amount of personal care expenditure that will keep the utility function non-negative.

b. Class intervals refer to GNP per capita at sample midpoints in 1970 U.S. dollars as given in column 5 of table 3-2. Jamaica is excluded.

Source: Lluch, Powell, and Williams (1977).

−0.2. Fifteen of the countries exhibit relatively inelastic demand. The results from aggregate data are qualitatively consistent with those from micro-level data—the demand for health care is relatively price inelastic.

Supply

The total cost of the service will obviously be affected if unit costs are responsive to any changes in the quantity of the service supplied. The magnitude of the impact depends upon whether the mix of health services is altered and also upon the presence of possible scale economies.

Information on the unit costs of providing health services is limited but useful. Unit cost varies significantly depending upon the level of service that is offered. Table 8-4 summarizes some of these costs for five countries. In Colombia and Malaysia, an inpatient day costs four to seven times more than an outpatient visit. For Peru, the average inpatient admission costs thirty times more than the average outpatient consultation. The mix of resources allocated to inpatient and outpatient care greatly affects the extent to which government can provide adequate health services.

There is no evidence that hospitals in developing countries experience a significant amount of scale economies. A comparison of unit costs of five Malaysian general hospitals of comparable quality indicates no perceptible downward trend in unit costs of inpatient days as the size of the facility increases (see table 8-5). There is even an upward trend with respect to outpatient visits. Although these comparisons are not strict because the controls for quality or differentials in input prices are rough, they still provide a pre-

Table 8-4. Public Unit Costs by Type of Medical Service

Country	Type of service	Unit recurrent and capital costs (1980 U.S. dollars)
Botswana	Outpatient visit	2–3
Colombia[a]	Outpatient visits	1.91
	Deliveries	2.20
	Operations	56.23
	Inpatient days	7.63
Malaysia[b]	Hospital inpatient	26.71
	Hospital outpatient	3.73
	Rural clinic unit	4.06
	Birth assistance by midwife	44.53
Peru	Inpatient (per admission)	
	Hospital	203.10
	Health center	126.40
Thailand	Outpatient visit	2–3

a. National health system hospitals.
b. Figures for peninsula only.
Sources: World Bank data for Botswana, Peru, and Thailand; Selowsky (1979) for Colombia; and Meerman (1979) for Malaysia.

Table 8-5. Unit Cost by Size of Hospital in Malaysia
(1974 ringgit)

Number of beds	Percentage of total expenditures spent on outpatients	Outpatient services (cost per visit)			Inpatient services (cost per inpatient day)		
		Recurrent	Capital	Total	Recurrent	Capital	Total
Satellite hospital							
41	35.3	1.50	0.98	2.48	17.33	15.54	32.87
75	31.3	3.00	2.42	5.42	15.61	15.54	31.15
81	23.1	4.48	3.28	7.76	20.63	14.25	34.88
200	16.8	1.97	2.27	4.24	13.02	19.64	32.66
206	23.4	1.69	1.47	3.16	13.13	16.22	29.35
244	25.3	3.27	4.27	7.54	10.46	17.99	28.45
260	26.2	3.30	4.20	7.50	13.74	22.61	36.35
General hospital							
368	16.1	2.98	—	4.94	21.96	—	41.03
789	16.3	3.52	—	6.29	17.33	—	36.54
903	25.6	3.25	—	5.92	17.92	—	35.03
1,067	16.7	3.75	—	6.69	—	—	—
2,016	16.8	5.69	—	8.63	23.70	—	37.28

— Not available.
Source: Heller (1975).

liminary indication that hospitals may not be natural monopolies that operate on the downward sloping portion of their cost curves.

Horton and Claquin (1983) report similar findings for rural health stations and hospitals in Bangladesh (see table 8-6). The long-run average cost per death averted is significantly lower for the smaller health service. Some conflicting evidence, however, prevents a firm conclusion regarding the shape of the average cost curve. For example, an analysis of a survey of seventy-five government hospitals in Kenya in 1975 concluded that economies of scale characterized the underlying cost structure of the sample facilities in the short run (Anderson 1980). Thus, hospitals are operating on the downward sloping portion of their short-run average cost curves. The study also found that for Kenya it would be more economical to increase output of existing facilities than to create new facilities.[1]

---

1. In the analysis of the impact of marginal fee increases on health services, alternative assumptions about elasticities were used.

Table 8-6. Unit Cost of Health Services in Rural Bangladesh
(costs in U.S. dollars)

	Matlab Type 1	Matlab Type 2	Ambulance	Sotaki
Number of users	10,618	10,618	4,359	891
Short-run average variable cost per patient	3.91	3.91	7.98	1.83
Short-run average cost per patient	15.56	16.68	11.47	3.10
Long-run average cost				
Per patient	15.65	16.77	12.80	3.36
Per severely ill patient	631.04	676.21	178.53	91.59
Cost per death averted	1,262.10	1,352.40	357.06	187.19

Note: Matlab and Sotaki are locations of treatment centers about ten miles apart. The Matlab type 2 differs from type 1 in having a microbiology laboratory and expatriate supervision and in using an existing *pucca* building rather than a rented *kutcha* building.

Source: Horton and Claquin (1983). Reprinted with permission; copyright 1983 Pergamon Journals Ltd.

Prices and Expansion

The efficiency gains from user charges for curative health care services depend, as in education, upon initial market characteristics. Although it is known that public health services are heavily subsidized in most developing countries, there is only anecdotal evidence of excess demand for them in some countries. Some facilities are underutilized (as in Malawi), and some provide very low quality service (as in Mali). Since these conditions could vary considerably from country to country, it is not possible to make general, concrete recommendations about user charges. This section will, instead, discuss their possible effects on expansion.

Excess Demand

The analytical and educational chapters have already outlined the conditions—excess demand or low quality—under which it would be beneficial to raise prices. Suppose that the total subsidy level or the budget allocation for health is fixed. If a less than optimal amount of funding is being provided, an increase in prices would generate resources that could be used to improve the quality of the system or to offer services to more people. Many clinics in Africa simply have no drugs (Birdsall and Chuhan 1983). If user fees were implemented and the revenue were used to purchase drugs, more people would receive better service, and efficiency would be improved. In many developing countries, however, prevailing policies may require that all fees from public health facilities revert to general government accounts.

If there is excess demand, moderate increases in user charges will increase rather than decrease the number of patients being served—even if quality is not enhanced to stimulate demand—because revenues can be used to hire more staff. The queue to obtain service will therefore shorten. (Estimates of the fee elasticity of demand indicate that the percentage decline in the queue would be less than the percentage rise in fee.) There are efficiency gains from shortening the queue: the first ones to leave will be those who are not willing to pay the moderate increase in fees. If these are people who are not very ill, then the fee hike will have increased the chance that the more seriously ill will be served. This allocation of resources is more efficient for society. If willingness to pay is a function of the severity of illness *and* income, then equity considerations arise. These are addressed below.

As table 8-7 indicates, a 10 percent increase in fee revenue, if all of it is used to finance expansion of a health service, can be expected to increase the amount of the service by about 1 percent at constant unit cost. This is because the bulk of the financing of present health services comes from subsidies. The ability of the service to expand is enhanced if there are scale economies. On average, a 10 percent fee increase could finance a service expansion of 2 percent if the cost elasticity estimate of -0.5 holds.

The policy prescription would, of course, be different if there were excess demand and the current level of the service exceeded the socially optimal amount. An example of this would be an ultramodern hospital facility that is costly to run and maintain per patient served. In this situation, if the total subsidy is fixed at a high level and cannot be reduced in the short run, fee revenue should not be used to expand the system. Instead it should be saved or unit fees should be lowered and the service rationed.

No Excess Demand

The effect of increased user charges on revenues depends upon whether the demand for the health service is a constraint. If there is excess demand, for example, then the entire percentage increase in fees could be used to expand the service. If not, an increase in fees would decrease demand. If demand for the services were relatively price inelastic, then revenues would increase.

Table 8-7. Impact of a 10 Percent Increase in Fees on Quantity of Public Health Services if Revenues Were Used to Expand Service

Country	Ratio of unit fee to unit recurrent cost	Percentage increase in health services if cost elasticity were 0.0	−0.5	−0.7
Africa				
Botswana	2.8	0.3	0.6	1.0
Burundi	4.0	0.4	0.9	1.5
Ghana	3.0	0.3	0.6	1.1
Lesotho	6.0	0.6	1.4	2.5
Malawi	3.0	0.3	0.6	1.1
Rwanda	7.0	0.8	1.6	3.0
Sudan	1.4	0.1	0.3	0.5
Togo	6.0	0.6	1.4	2.5
Zimbabwe	2.2	0.2	0.5	0.8
Asia				
Indonesia	15.5	1.8	4.5	10.7
Malaysia	18.0	2.2	5.6	15.0
Pakistan	2.5	0.3	0.5	0.9
Philippines	6.8	0.7	1.6	2.9
Sri Lanka	0.7	0.1	0.1	0.2
Middle East				
Jordan	13.2	1.5	3.6	7.9
Tunisia	2.0	0.2	0.4	0.7
Latin America				
Colombia	28.4	4.0	13.1	177.5
Peru	8.0	0.9	1.9	3.6
Average	7.3	0.9	2.2	13.0

Note: The persistence of excess demand is assumed in these calculations.
Source: Calculated from table 2-3, using equation C-18 from appendix C.

Suppose that a country maintains the equilibrium level of services through a mixture of subsidies and fee revenues. If the country were committed to meeting all demand and subsidies were cut by 10 percent, what should the fee increase be? Table 8-8 shows that relatively modest increases in fees could compensate for the subsidy reduction. Even if demand had an elasticity of −0.5, a 2.8 percent increase in fees could, on average, finance the 10 percent loss in a subsidy allocation and still maintain equilibrium. The consequent decline in utilization would be about 1 percent.

Such a fee increase would have very little effect on average household expenditures. For example, fee payments in Malaysia account for 0.1 percent of

Table 8-8. Impact of a 10 Percent Decline in Subsidies on Fees, Quantity of Public Health Care, and Household Payments to Minimize Social Losses

Country	Unit fee as percentage of unit cost	Percentage fee increase if demand elasticity were −0.5	Percentage fee increase if demand elasticity were −1.0	Percentage decline in utilization if fees rise and demand elasticity were −0.5	Percentage decline in utilization if fees rise and demand elasticity were −1.0
Africa					
Botswana	2.8	3.0	2.6	−1.5	−2.6
Burundi	4.0	2.2	2.0	−1.1	−2.0
Ghana	3.0	2.9	2.5	−1.4	−2.5
Lesotho	6.0	1.5	1.4	−0.8	−1.4
Malawi	3.0	2.9	2.5	−1.4	−2.5
Rwanda	7.0	1.3	1.3	−0.7	−1.3
Sudan	1.4	5.3	4.2	−2.6	−4.2
Togo	6.0	1.5	1.4	−0.8	−1.4
Zimbabwe	2.2	3.7	3.1	−1.9	−3.1
Asia					
Indonesia	15.5	0.6	0.6	−0.3	−0.6
Malaysia	18.0	0.5	0.5	−0.3	−0.5
Pakistan	2.5	3.3	2.9	−1.7	−2.9
Philippines	6.8	1.4	1.3	−0.7	−1.3
Sri Lanka	0.7	8.3	5.9	−4.2	−5.9
Middle East					
Jordan	13.2	0.7	0.7	−0.4	−0.7
Tunisia	2.0	4.0	3.3	−2.0	−3.3
Latin America					
Colombia	28.4	0.3	0.3	−0.2	−0.3
Peru	8.0	1.2	1.1	−0.6	−1.1
Average	7.2	2.5	2.1	−1.2	−2.1

Note: Although there is anecdotal evidence that many of the countries in tables 8-7 and 8-8 confront excess demand for health services, for illustrative purposes it is assumed in the calculations shown here that each system is in equilibrium.

Source: Calculated from table 2-3, using equation C-11 from appendix C.

household income. A 19 percent increase in household payments would mean that the proportion of household income for medical services would have to rise to 0.12 percent—an almost imperceptible increase. Even for the lowest-income households, if demand elasticities were constant across income groups, the percentage of household income spent on publicly provided health care would rise from 0.36 percent to only 0.43 percent. Data for other countries are not available.

The calculations made above assume constant unit costs. It is possible, however, that health services would exhibit increasing returns to scale. In this case lower utilization would result in higher unit costs. Since the evidence on the extent of scale economies in the health services is even less than what is available for education, further calculations of alternative assumptions about costs are not presented.

Prices and Efficiency

Aside from mobilizing resources to expand services, increased cost recovery could also improve efficiency within the health system. If health services are offered for free across the board, the demand for any service will be very heavy. The providers will be confronted by individuals with a range of maladies, some of which require immediate and sustained attention while others might require little or no care at all. It is difficult to determine who should be given priority access. Individuals would have an incentive to overutilize a free system.

Of course, not all who demand immediate attention would get it. Free services are frequently rationed to match budgetary restraints. The most commonly used rationing device is the queue, which limits service to those who come first. To a certain extent, the cost of waiting is a private cost that may deter some individuals from seeking unnecessary health care. It is an inefficient allocative device, however, if some services have to be provided expeditiously. Increased cost recovery for curative care would deter those with minor complaints from seeking unnecessary care.

With uncertain and large health expenditures, such as hospitalization charges, it would not be efficient to rely solely on fees to finance services rendered. Individuals cannot be expected to save large amounts of money simply because some day they may need to finance a large hospital bill. Many could not mobilize these amounts, and if they could it would be better if they pooled their resources to minimize the risks through insurance schemes.[2]

In insurance schemes, individuals pool their resources into a fund from which those who are sick can withdraw. A premium, paid regularly regardless of the occurrence of an illness, is charged to all the participants. Because not everyone will need assistance with medical expenses at the same time, the fund will be able to finance substantial costs, such as those for hospitalization, for some of the scheme's members.

---

2. The complex topic of insurance and its role in cost recovery is treated only superficially here. For a more comprehensive treatment and possible applications to developing countries, see Besley, Bevan, and Collier (1985).

Insurance schemes suffer from two inherent drawbacks. First, there is a tendency in insurance markets for people to buy insurance when they know that they are likely to become ill. When these people do actually become ill, their health care is paid by the insurance. As more people become ill, the total cost of providing insurance increases. This causes insurers to increase the prices of their premiums. Expensive premiums deter healthy, low-risk people from purchasing insurance. As a result, there may not be enough healthy people contributing to the premium pool to pay for the expenses of the sick. Under these conditions, insurers spend more than they receive in revenues from premiums. This problem, called adverse selection, might be resolved through compulsory public health insurance. Private insurance might also be effective if made compulsory.

Second, insurance providers, whether public or private, must confront the problem of "moral hazard." The insured who falls ill consumes more health care than is needed. Once the premium is paid, there is nothing to hinder a patient from getting more services than are necessary. A fee for service together with a premium-based financing scheme might lessen this problem by discouraging overutilization.

Another type of moral hazard arises when health service providers prescribe more treatment than is required. For example, the private sector may use capital-intensive techniques when simpler ones would do, and prescribe more treatment than is necessary. Overtreatment occurs when uninformed patients fail to recognize that they are receiving unnecessary tests or medicines. It also occurs when insurance systems are heavily subsidized or charge no premiums. Patients then have no incentive to minimize costs, and physicians can prescribe extra services and gain financially, especially if they are paid directly for the services they render. A fee-for-service system would only partially resolve this problem because patients cannot shop for the most cost-effective treatment—they lack information about the performance of various medical services. In addition, physicians' practices should be regularly monitored to control excessive treatments. One way to do this without placing an undue informational burden on the user would be through competition among providers in private systems. In public systems, incomes of physicians might be prepaid or based upon how well they minimize costs, as they are in health maintenance organizations. Because the cost of treatments would come out of their own budgets, they would have an incentive to keep costs down.

The few reviews of the use of insurance in developing countries show that most medical insurance is provided as a component of social insurance. Higher-income countries in Latin America provide extensive social insurance coverage, while lower-income countries, which account for only 22 percent of the region's total population, provide only limited coverage (see table 8-9).

Table 8-9. Care under Social Insurance in Sixteen Latin American Countries, ca. 1977

Country (in order of per capita income)	Percentage of population covered	Dominant pattern of medical care[a]	Equal benefits for dependents	Per capita cost of medical care social insurance (U.S. dollars)	Percentage of social insurance financing from[b] Workers	Employers	Government	Health care costs as percentage of GDP Social insurance	Public health	Percentage of total social insurance devoted to medical care
Higher-income countries										
Argentina	80	Indirect	Yes	—	38.0	51.8	0	—	—	20
Brazil	83	Indirect	Yes	23	—	—	—	1.4	0.7	23
Costa Rica	82	Direct	Yes	51	25.7	48.5	2.1	3.8	0.6	52
Mexico	56	Direct	Yes	—	—	—	—	—	—	—
Panama	47	Direct	Yes	74	29.5	53.2	4.1	3.1	1.5	33
Uruguay	47	Indirect	No	14	28.6	47.5	7.5	0.5	0.9	5
Venezuela	30	Direct	Yes	59	23.9	47.8	15.3	0.7	1.5	37
Lower-income countries										
Bolivia	26	Direct	Yes	52	32.3	53.9	0	1.3	1.0	39
Colombia	10	Direct	No	49	24.3	58.2	5.4	0.9	0.8	31
Dominican Republic	4	Direct	No	73	16.6	64.4	0	0.4	1.2	32
Ecuador	5	Direct	No	89	—	—	—	0.7	1.3	—
El Salvador	5	Direct	No	52	26.7	63.7	0	0.6	1.4	29
Guatemala	14	Direct	No	25	30.3	55.6	12.6	0.5	0.8	31
Honduras	7	Direct	No	48	—	—	—	0.8	1.6	—
Paraguay	13	Direct	Yes	—	—	—	—	—	—	—
Peru	12	Direct	No	36	—	—	—	0.8	1.0	—

— Not available.

a. Direct pattern implies a social insurance fund that operates medical facilities itself. Indirect pattern implies one that merely finances and regulates purchases from private or public providers.

b. The sum of these three columns, when subtracted from 100, yields the percentage of social insurance financing from capital and other income.

Source: Various tables from Zschock (1986).

Coverage, primarily for urban workers, is financed through wage deductions and subsidies from employers and the government.

A few forms of medical insurance are linked to public health facilities in developing countries. Donaldson (undated) evaluated such a scheme in Nepal and concluded that adverse selection was indeed a problem since sicker households tended to enroll in the plan with the highest premium. The two-part tariff of premium plus fees, however, seemed to work well in controlling utilization.

Insurance may be relevant only for middle- and high-income groups because of the high risks in insuring and collecting premiums from the lowest-income groups. The most visible formal insurance schemes are medical coverage under social security programs and employer plans serving urban workers, but other, more broadly defined varieties of insurance are employer-based schemes serving workers on agricultural estates, community-financed schemes, and cooperatives. In these smaller bodies, the costs of monitoring risk and collection may be lower than for larger groups. The ability to pool risks, however, declines with size. It may be efficient to subsidize insurance targeted to low-income groups. In fact, some analysts (see Culyer 1980) have argued that the public sector should provide the insurance, if, because of scale economies, it incurs lower costs than does the private sector. Public sector domination, however, would not be the only efficient solution even if scale economies did exist. Regulated private monopolies are also an alternative.

Prices and Equity

Present subsidy systems do not lead to equal consumption of some types of health services. The main problem is that subsidized health insurance schemes tend to cover primarily urban wage earners in the formal sector. In Colombia, for example, making the system of hospitals in the social security system (which serves employees in the private sector) pay for itself would affect mostly the higher-income groups.

Although differential charges among income groups could improve progressivity, this practice is still not widespread. There is more room for differential charges between rural and urban areas. In Colombia and Malaysia, for example, urban areas receive a larger share of the health services.

Tables 8-10 and 8-11 present the distribution of costs and payments for Malaysian and Colombian households. Payments are the average amounts that households of each income group pay for services. These figures also depend upon use of the services by the average household in each income group. The cost figures are the proportion of income that the average household would have to pay if it had to incur the full amount of recurrent

Table 8-10. Affordability of Health Care in Malaysia: Payments and Social Costs as Percentage of Household Income by Income Quintile

Type of service	Income quintile	Frequency of use[a]	Fee payment	Recurrent social cost[b]	Total social cost per household[c]
Inpatient days	1	2.4	0.27	3.48	6.18
	2	3.5	0.23	2.89	5.18
	3	1.3	0.06	0.78	1.38
	4	3.0	0.09	1.22	2.17
	5	2.5	0.03	0.45	0.80
	Overall	2.5	0.08	1.00	1.78
Public hospital outpatient visits	1	5.3	0.03	1.20	1.85
	2	4.9	0.02	0.64	0.98
	3	5.5	0.02	0.50	0.78
	4	4.5	0.01	0.28	0.43
	5	4.0	0.003	0.11	0.18
	Overall	4.8	0.01	0.29	0.45
		Mean monthly household income (ringgit)			
Combined public medical services[d]	1	129.3	0.36	5.99	10.40
	2	223.4	0.28	4.26	7.39
	3	315.5	0.10	1.61	2.99
	4	460.8	0.12	1.77	3.17
	5	1,037.0	0.10	1.48	2.80
	Overall	471.8	0.10	1.48	2.80

a. Number of inpatient days or number of public hospital outpatient visits.

b. For inpatient days, the recurrent social cost equals unit current cost times the mean frequency of use (mean number of inpatient days per household, for all peninsular Malaysia households), divided by the mean annual household income for each income group. A similar method is used for outpatient visits.

c. Mean current cost and mean capital service cost per household.

d. Includes the preceding categories plus outpatient visits to rural clinics.

Source: Meerman (1979).

Table 8-11. Affordability of Public Health Services in Colombia

Income quintile	Annual household income (Colombian pesos)	Cost of providing National Health Service's hospital service and health center per household	National Health Service cost per household as percentage of household income[a]
1	10,368	514	5.0
2	17,820	440	2.5
3	25,032	393	1.6
4	36,912	321	0.9
5	104,388	210	0.2
Overall	38,904	376	1.0

a. Extra private costs, such as those for transport to the facility, are not included.
Source: Selowsky (1979).

costs. Mean payments and social costs are lower for the higher-income quintiles because they tend to use public services less frequently than do lower-income groups. For Malaysia, payments for combined health services take up an average one-tenth of 1 percent of household income. If the average household were to bear the full burden of the recurrent costs of all publicly provided health services, it would have to devote 1.6 percent of household income. If it were to bear the burden of all costs, it would have to devote almost 3 percent of income. The latter figure ranges from 1 percent for high-income groups to 11 percent for low-income groups.

If households in Colombia had to pay the full cost of the National Health Service, the healthier ones would pay 0.2 percent of their income, the average ones would pay 1.6 percent, and the poorer ones would pay 5 percent. Clearly, fee payments comprise only a small portion of household income, even among the poorest.

9

Feasibility of Policy Change

COSTS ARE ASSOCIATED with any policy change. These costs, whether economic or political, can be an effective barrier to implementation. Even if overall gains from any changes outweigh the costs, including those of putting them in place, policymakers must be able to identify potential losers—and to know whether they can effectively block reform. The policy package must include measures to address these issues.

The relative importance of implementation issues will vary among countries. Thus, it is beyond the scope of this book to detail the steps toward implementation. It is instructive, however, to discuss briefly some general principles.

The efficiency gains from increased user charges hinge on the ability of governments to use the revenues thus generated within the social sectors. The ultimate disposition of the funds, however, depends upon those who are given control over them. Funds collected at the school or health unit may have to be turned over to central authorities. In some governments, the funds may have to be surrendered to the central fiscal authorities, which may allocate them outside the sector. The issue is further complicated in federal systems where the central government may be responsible for one type of service, such as higher education, and local authorities for other types, such as primary and secondary education. Thus, it is probably preferable that the funds from user fees be controlled by the authorities that control the social sectors so that they do not have to be first transferred to the fiscal authorities for distribution later.

There is very little information on the costs of collecting fees in education or health. Nevertheless, it has been frequently argued that it would be prohibitively expensive to collect charges directly. Since there is a paucity of hard evidence, it is not possible to compute the costs of collection per dollar of revenue. This would certainly be a fruitful area of future research. It is possible, however, to speculate on what such an investigation should encompass.

Just as there are administrative costs in charging and collecting fees, so are there costs in levying and collecting taxes. If it can be argued that the marginal cost of an additional dollar of tax collected is zero in administrative terms (since taxes are collected anyway), the argument must also hold for an additional dollar of fees collected. More important, however, are the distortionary effects of collecting revenue through taxes. Developing countries rely to a large extent on taxes that drive a wedge between the price that agents observe and the true scarcity value of a commodity. Income taxes are only a small proportion of total government revenue. Other indirect taxes and trade duties may cause efficiency losses and may be regressive. Moreover, because of the uncertainties in the budget-making process, the price of obtaining a dollar of revenue to cover recurrent costs may be greater than the forgone resources (USAID 1982). These costs have to be weighed with those of direct collection from users, and it is not clear beforehand which will be greater.

There is, of course, substantial room for improvement in the collection system for user fees, although the record of the education sector in enforcing existing rules is better than that of other social sectors, such as health (Ainsworth 1984). An alternative to central government control is to place more emphasis on localized collection efforts. In this way each community decides how much education or health it will provide and is primarily responsible for paying for it. Since it may be difficult for central authorities to collect from individuals, the distribution of subsidies will be left up to each community. But communities would, to a larger extent, be self-supporting. There are at least three reasons why this system may be appropriate. First, as already mentioned, it may be cheaper, since the money will have to go through fewer agencies before it is spent. Second, local authorities will have more of an incentive to collect charges if they are certain that the funds will be used locally. Third, users will be more inclined to pay a fee if they believe that it will be used to improve local facilities. These advantages would have to be weighed in each case and would depend upon the resources at the local level for handling financial transactions and the degree of inequality across localities that might result.

A frequent argument against increasing user charges for potentially large investments, such as education, has been that household economies in the least developed countries (particularly in subsistence rural areas within them) are not monetized. As a result, it is virtually impossible to mobilize resources from users.

The lack of a monetized economy should not, in itself, be a significant barrier to transferring greater responsibility for financing to users. Private resources may be mobilized in kind. In particular, communities frequently contribute labor to the capital costs and, in some instances, recurrent costs of building and running schools in some African countries.

In education, the best-documented examples are the Kenyan harambee schools. As of 1981–82, approximately 20 percent (more than 82,000 students) of secondary school enrollment in Kenya was in unsubsidized harambee schools. Another 20 percent was in assisted harambee schools, where public subsidies accounted on average for only about 18 percent of unit costs per student (Bertrand and Griffin 1983, 42). Thus, some 40 percent of Kenyan secondary school students were enrolled in schools where private assistance was mobilized not only through cash contributions to cover operating costs, but also through local materials and voluntary labor in school-building. Schools are organized by local committees that continue to guide their management. The committee determines the type of support that parents will give the school (for instance, by arranging work days for construction tasks). Usually monetary "fines" are imposed in lieu of labor. The committee also keeps the parents informed about school affairs. One example is the Kenyatta High School in an isolated part of the Nyeri district, where 4,000 residents were mobilized mainly to contribute their own labor in September 1965. Material costs were minimized (to about half what the government would have incurred) by making the design simple and by using local materials (Roth 1987, chap. 2).

Other innovative financing schemes are based on income-generating activities by students and their families. In many elementary schools in Africa, students maintain income-earning farms. In one Rwandan school that has only one plot, eight- and nine-year-old students were able to grow $120 worth of potatoes—six times what the school received in government grants—and the profits were used to purchase equipment (Kulakow, Brace, and Morrill 1978, 15). There is little evidence, however, to determine whether such efforts at school-based production are generally successful.

In the health sector, a review of seventy community-based health schemes worldwide also describes various innovations (Stinson and American Public Health Association 1982). Aside from fees for service, voluntary labor and payments in output (as in China) are commonly used to contribute to capital costs as well as to compensate community health workers. The success of these schemes in maintaining the financial viability of the system depends upon the commitment of the community leaders and their resourcefulness in mobilizing support.

The political feasibility of user charges obviously must be considered in adopting policies. Since this is likely to vary widely from country to country, it is up to the practitioner to decide how important each factor is. Great resistance to the imposition of fees would argue for a gradual introduction. A more important consideration in cutting subsidies is the identity of the main recipients of the subsidies; they are sometimes in a position to decide or influence such policies.

Political acceptability and administrative feasibility can be partially accommodated by phasing in the policy change gradually. The precise sequence and timing would vary from country to country. For the health field, Birdsall (1985) suggests this sequence: (1) introduction of or increase in hospital charges for private patients; (2) greater efforts to recover costs from those with medical insurance, including user charges and premiums; (3) fees levied on patients who bypass an initial examination in countries where a referral system exists; (4) introduction of or increase in other inpatient charges (for meals, visitors, and special services); and (5) introduction of or increase in outpatient fees.

If possible, governments should also encourage the growth of insurance markets to cover a wider range of people. Many countries have successfully implemented such schemes. In education, policies to diminish students' living allowance could precede actual increases in tuition. At the same time, measures could be taken to institute student credit schemes (Mingat, Tan, and Hoque 1984).

Perhaps the most telling argument for the feasibility of pricing policies to mobilize resources in the social sectors is that nations have begun to implement them, according to recent studies conducted by the World Bank. For example, in education, university subsidies were reduced in Morocco in 1982 by half, with the exception of those to students from very poor homes. Similar policies are being considered in Ghana. In Malawi and Tanzania, fees were increased at the secondary level. (See World Bank 1986 for a more comprehensive list.)

Birdsall (1985) documents some recent attempts to raise fee revenue in health systems, including some being financed by the World Bank. For example, charges for medicines are being implemented in the Gambia and China; hospital fees are being charged in ten countries (Burundi, Cameroon, China, Ghana, Indonesia, Lesotho, Pakistan, Philippines, Rwanda, and Togo); and outpatients pay consultation fees in Botswana, Burundi, Indonesia, Lesotho, Pakistan, Rwanda, and Zimbabwe.

Appendixes

A

A Review of Alternative Pricing Policies

THE ARGUMENTS BELOW assume that prices elsewhere in the economy are given. They are based on partial equilibrium analysis.

General Pricing Rules

Figure A-1 depicts marginal cost pricing if there are no externalities or other market imperfections. For the representative consumer the private marginal benefit (PMB) equals the social marginal benefit (SMB). As a person is satiated, PMB is assumed to decrease with each additional unit. The private marginal cost (PMC) equals the social marginal cost (SMC) and, for presentational purposes, is assumed to be constant with each additional unit. At a price $p = p_1$, SMB = PMB > PMC = SMC, and consumption at $q = q_1$ would be suboptimal, since the value to society of an extra unit of consumption of q_1 exceeds the cost to society of providing it. At a price $p = p_2$, SMB = PMB < PMC = SMC, and consumption at $q = q_2$ would be "overconsumption," since the value to society of the extra unit consumed at q_2 is less than the cost of providing the extra unit. Efficiency is reached at $p = p_0$, where p_0 = SMB = PMB = PMC = SMC for consumption at q_0. The efficiency losses at $p = p_1$ can be measured by the extent of the "underconsumption" (the difference between q_0 and q_1) times the amount by which marginal social benefit exceeds marginal social cost at each q. This would be area x. The efficiency losses at $p = p_2$ would, by a similar argument, be equal to area y.

The analysis is easily extended if there is more than one individual. The individual PMB curves are first summed horizontally to form the aggregate PMB. In figure A-2 this aggregate curve is shown by $PMB_A + PMB_B = PMB$. Then the analysis proceeds in the same manner as above, where total consumption would be q_0.

Figure A-1. Marginal Cost Pricing without Externalities

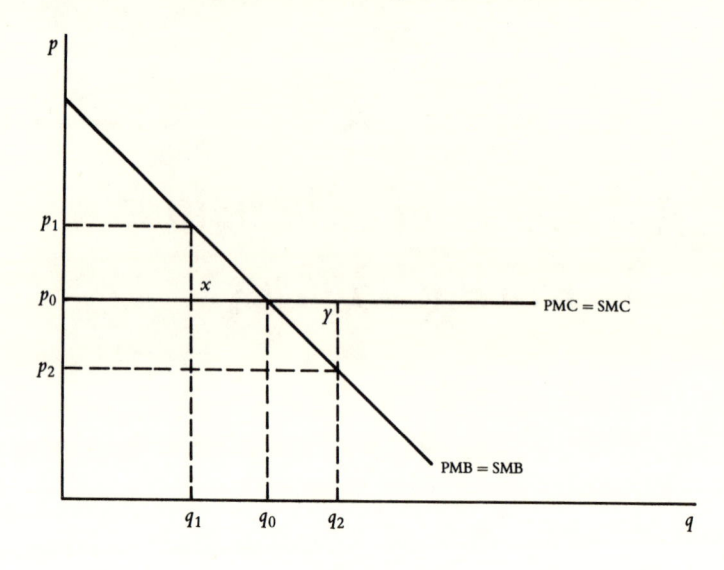

Figure A-2. Marginal Cost Pricing without Externalities, with Multiple Types of Demanders

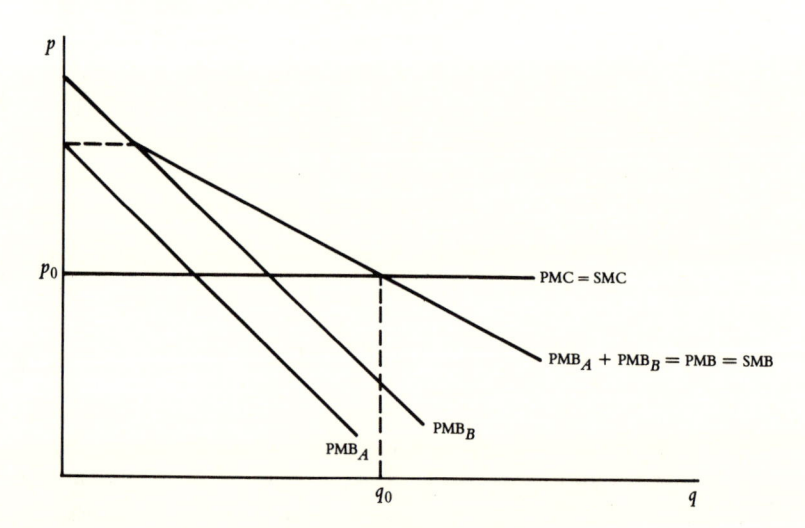

The pricing rule in the presence of externalities depends on their extent. In figure A-3, if externalities imply that the social marginal benefit is SMB_0, the price charged should be $p = p_1 < p_0$, the full cost-recovery price, to ensure a socially optimal level of consumption q_1. If user charges were used to fully recover costs, there would be underconsumption by the amount $q_0 q_1$. The difference between p_0 and p_1 would have to be financed by subsidies. If SMB_1 applies, prices should be zero to obtain optimal consumption at q_2. For any social marginal benefit schedule beyond SMB_1, public authorities would have to pay the consumer a certain amount to induce consumption at an optimal level.

Basic Needs

The basic needs level of consumption can be interpreted as a minimum amount that society or the policymaker considers desirable. In this case, the optimal level of subsidies can be analyzed as in the externalities case (although the "externalities" in this case are not as tangible and extend only up to a certain amount). A consumer whose private marginal benefit is less than the social marginal cost at the minimum amount of consumption would have to be subsidized by that difference. For other consumers whose optimal

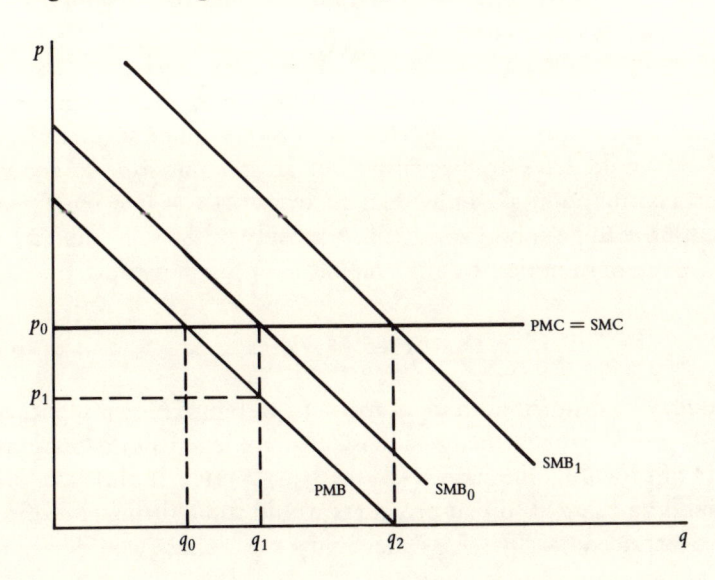

Figure A-3. Marginal Cost Pricing with Externalities

Figure A-4. Basic Needs

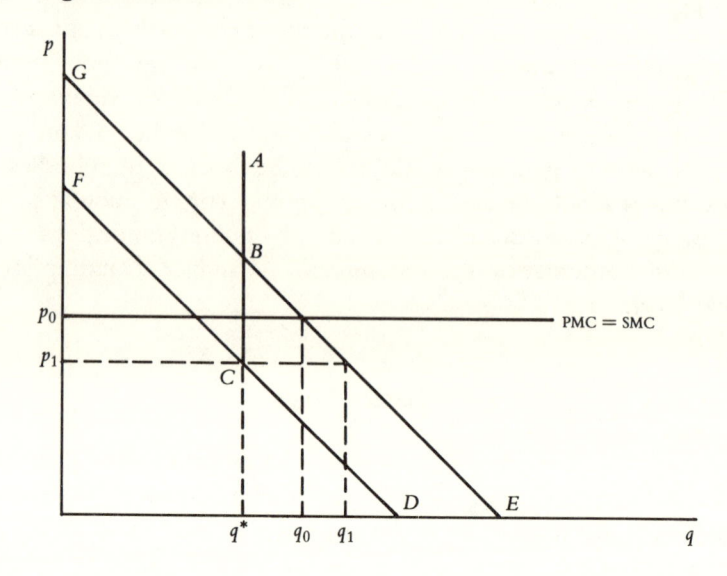

consumption level is beyond the minimum amount prescribed by society, the provision of a similar subsidy (which would occur in any uniform pricing scheme) would lead to overconsumption. Thus, the basic needs argument is one for differential pricing. The only individuals who should be charged a zero price are those for whom the private marginal benefit of another unit of consumption is exactly nil at the minimum amount of consumption that is prescribed for society. Figure A-4 illustrates this case.

Let q^* = the minimum amount of consumption considered desirable by the policymaker. In effect, this implies that the SMB is line segment ACD for an individual whose private marginal benefit is PMB = line segment FCD. Individual A would have to be subsidized an amount $p_0 p_1$ to induce the minimum consumption q^*. Individual B, whose PMB = line segment GBE, would not have to be subsidized at all. A subsidy of the same amount would imply an overconsumption by the amount $q_0 q_1$ for individual B.

Distorted Markets

There may be distortions in input markets. In figure A-5, if inputs are underpriced, providers incur marginal costs that are less than the marginal cost to society of providing the service (SMC = SMC_1 > PMC). In this case, prices ($p = p_1$) would be charged so that providers would run a financial profit. If inputs are overpriced, SMC = SMC_2 < PMC and $p - p_2$. There would have to be a subsidy $p_0 p_2$.

Figure A-5. Distortions in Input Markets

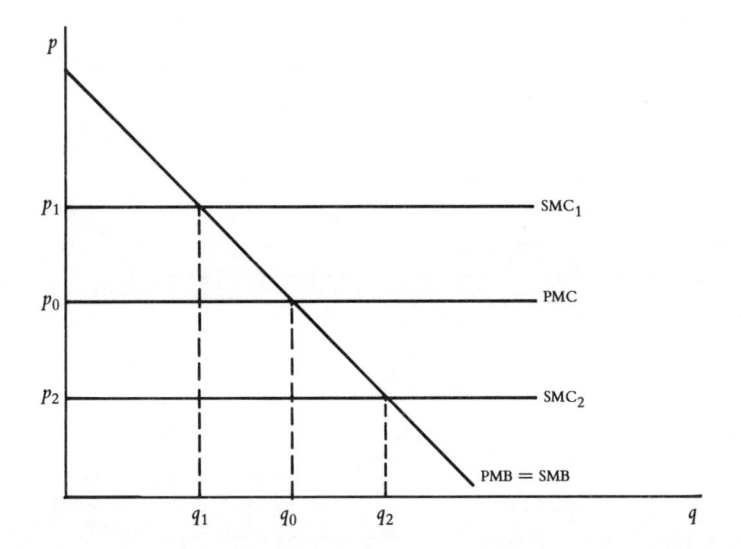

Alternatively, there could be distortions in output markets. If university graduates, for example, were paid a wage that exceeded the value of their marginal product, then the benefit to society from another graduate would be less than the private benefit. In this case, the provider should charge p_1 and run a financial profit to induce an optimal level of consumption q_1 (see figure A-6).

Figure A-6. Distortions in Output Markets

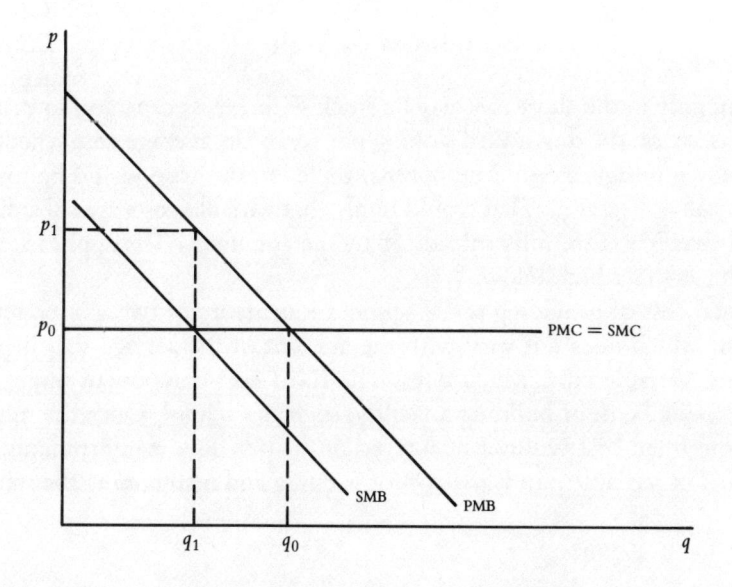

Figure A-7. Pricing of Nonexclusive Goods

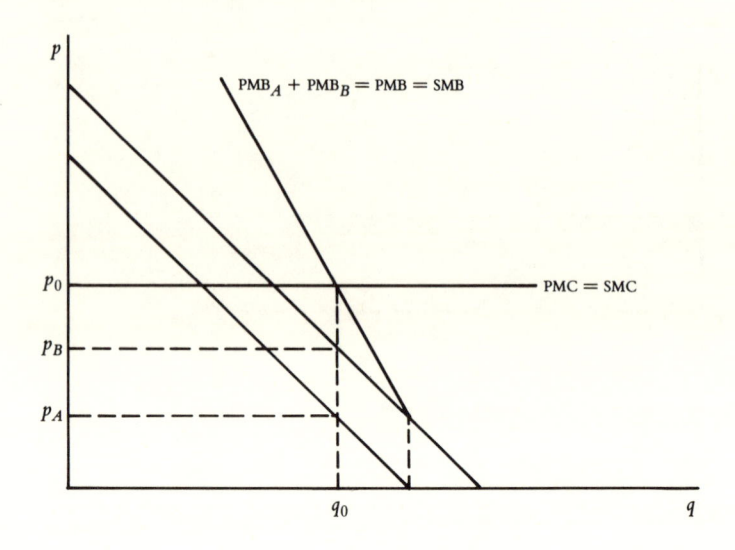

Pure Public Goods

Pure public goods imply that the consumption by one individual does not exclude the consumption by another. Thus, the total willingness to pay for any unit of the commodity is the vertical sum of individuals' willingness to pay (such as PMB_A and PMB_B in figure A-7). Optimal price will differ by individual (p_B and p_A).

Economies of Scale

A monopoly in the short run may be stuck with excess capacity, so that its operations are on the downward sloping portion of its average cost schedule. This is shown in figure A-8. The optimal policy in this case would be to ensure that SMB = SMC at q_0. That would imply that variable costs are subsidized by s_1 and fixed costs are fully subsidized by the amount s_2. The application of this model is described below.

The total cost of providing social services is made up of two components: fixed cost, which does not vary with the amount of the service that is produced, and variable cost, which does. The fixed cost component might include the capital cost of building a facility, such as a school. Once the school is built, the fixed cost will not be altered no matter how many students are educated. The variable cost is the cost of running and maintaining the school

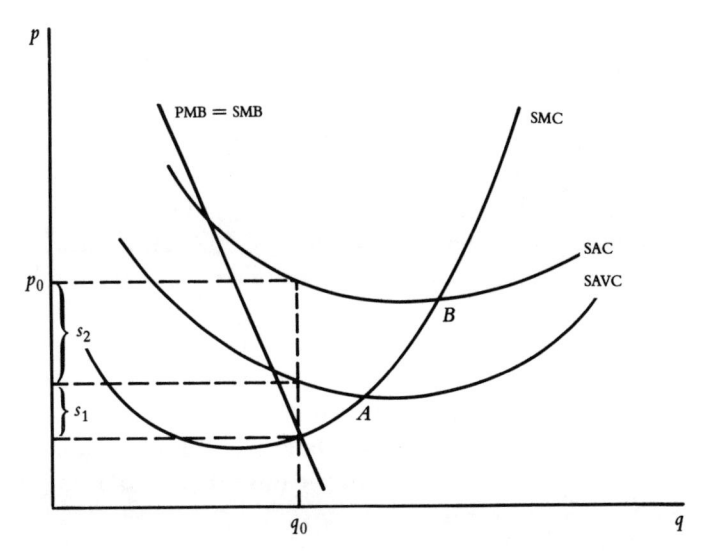

Figure A-8. Pricing When Capital Is Indivisible and Average Costs Are Decreasing

and varies with the size of the school. To educate more students at a given quality, more labor and maintenance expenditures must be made. These considerations imply that, in the short run, average costs are U-shaped. In other words, for low levels of output, average costs are declining because of the effect of decreasing average fixed costs; at higher levels of output, average costs are rising because more output is being squeezed out while at least some inputs (capital) are held fixed. For a school with low enrollment, average costs per student fall and then eventually rise as the level of enrollment increases.

If the school were a publicly owned monopoly that attempted to provide the socially optimal number of places and if it faced a low enough demand for its places, the school might be operating on the downward sloping portion of its average cost curve in the short run. Such a situation is shown in figure A-8, where the hypothetical school faces a short-run average cost of SAC and an average variable cost of SAVC. Marginal cost is labeled SMC. If long-run average costs (LAC, not shown in the figure) were constant and tangent to SAC at B, the school would be suffering from overcapacity since it could probably do with a smaller capital stock.[1] Given that overcapacity because of, say,

---

1. The SAC of such a (smaller) school would be tangent to long-run average cost where LAC intersects PMB.

indivisibilities, the optimal pricing solution would be to fully subsidize the average fixed cost (by s_2) and charge p_0 only to recover a portion of the variable cost (Saunders and Warford 1976; de Ferranti 1983). The overall average subsidy would be $s_1 + s_2$ in figure A-8. These assumptions would be more likely to hold for facilities where fixed costs were relatively large, such as hospitals and urban schools.

The above considerations apply if providers can minimize costs in the short run but not in the long run. But the same arguments hold even under long-run cost minimization if there are economies of scale in the long run. As the system expands and more schools or health facilities are built, long-run average costs decline. Although such a scenario might not be true in the rural areas (where long-run average costs may increase because of the difficulty in serving a dispersed population), it probably is in urban areas. An expanding system may be able to obtain discounts in unit costs of inputs. In addition, once land was bought, newer multistory buildings would be established on the same site and thus lead to expansion without the costs of negotiating new land leases. The appropriate pricing strategy in this case would be to subsidize costs equal to the difference between long-run average costs and marginal costs. A full recovery policy would lead to underconsumption.

An alternative that does not require a subsidy is a two-part pricing scheme. The first part is a lump sum periodic payment for the portion of costs above marginal costs that would have to be recovered. This lump sum payment is presumed to be insufficient to deter consumption, which is determined by the second part of the tariff, a user charge that is based on marginal cost.

B

Pricing Policies under Budgetary Restraints

THIS APPENDIX DERIVES the optimal allocation when some parameters are fixed at levels that make the first-best infeasible.

Fixed Subsidy Allocations

Suppose that central governments set the total subsidy level (budget allocation) at S. To simplify the analysis, it is assumed that average social cost is constant at c (see figure B-1). This cost is the sum of privately incurred costs c_p and the cost to the provider of the service. D_p and D_s are the marginal willingness to pay schedules for the user and the society, respectively. Thobani's (1983) iso-subsidy locus, which is the locus of combinations of unit subsidies and quantities that exhaust S, is the curve S_0. Thus, $S_0/c = q_0$ is the amount of the service that would be provided if the service were free. The optimal subsidy level is at S^*, which is the level of subsidy that would just finance the difference between the total cost of providing the optimal level of output, q^*, and the amount that can be recovered through fee payments.

As Thobani shows, for a subsidy that is S_1, which is less than S^*, the price p^*, which would have been optimal for the allocation S^*, would entail a loss of area ADE and excess demand $q_0 q^*$. Under the tighter S_1 budgetary constraint, the optimal policy would be to raise prices to p_2 and use the additional revenue to expand the service until the market clears at q_1. This would imply a smaller social loss at BFE. But if the initial price level is above p_1, at a subsidy level S_1, this will cause an oversupply of the service, even though the level of subsidy is "too small." The amount actually consumed would be less than the optimal amount. Thus, prices should be lowered and demand stimulated until equilibrium is reached.

If the subsidy level is greater than the optimal level (say, at S_2), any price equal to or above the first-best price would result in excess supply. Any ex-

Figure B-1. Pricing Policies under Budgetary Constraints

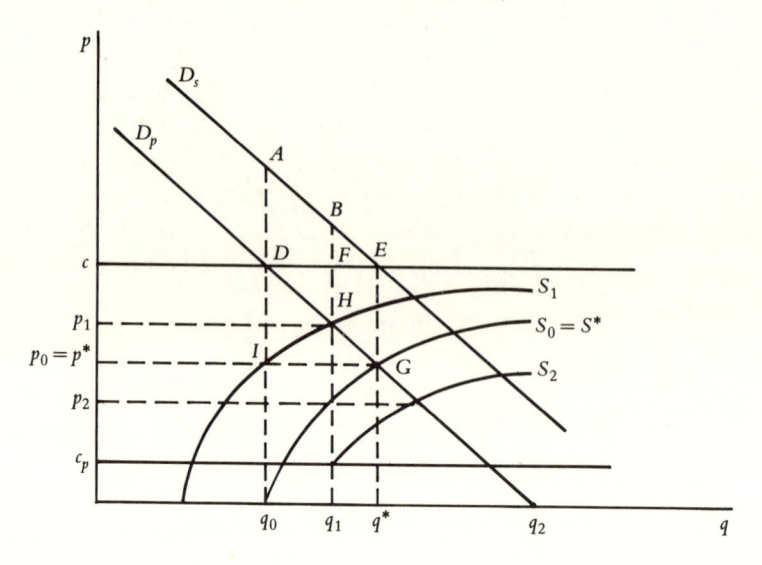

cess supply beyond the optimal level of consumption is wasteful, since at a lower price more benefits could be reaped with increased demand and with fewer resources. Equilibrium in this case would be reached beyond the first-best consumption level, q^*. Society could do better, however, by providing fewer services at a lower price even though excess demand will be caused. The optimal price level will be at the first-best consumption level but at a low enough price to use up all of the excess subsidy. (The alternative is to run a budget surplus.) Excess demand of q^*q_2 is optimal! This occurs precisely because the amount of the subsidy is too large. If there is to be rationing, it is crucial that the policy allocate places to the ones who value it the most—those with the highest rate of return in education and those with the greatest need in health.

Fixed Prices

Sometimes political constraints require governments to set prices at a certain level. In this case, the appropriate subsidy policy to follow depends on the fixed level of prices. If $p = p^*$, then subsidies should be adjusted until equilibrium is reached. If there is excess demand at $S = S_1$, subsidies should be increased until the market clears at $S = S_1$ and q^*. If there is excess supply at S_2, subsidies should be cut until $S = S^*$ and $q = q^*$.

The story differs if prices are fixed at $p \neq p^*$. If $p = p_1 > p^*$, then subsidies should be adjusted until market clearing is reached. For example, at p_1, a subsidy allocation S^* would be too large and imply excess supply if all funds from fee payments and the subsidy were spent on q. Thus, S^* should be lowered to S_1. If $p = p_2 < p^*$, subsidies should be adjusted only until q^* is provided (at $S = S_1^*$). This implies that, even if excess demand were observed, subsidies should exceed S_2. Excess demand of q^*q_2 would be optimal.

If p were set at a ceiling $\bar{p}$, rather than a level at which prices were fixed, the analysis would not greatly change. If $\bar{p} \leqslant p^*$, the conclusion described above holds. If the maximum price were set above p^*, then the appropriate subsidy policy would revert to that of obtaining the first-best solution, which is now feasible.

C

The Algebra of User Fees

Impact of Changes in Subsidy Allocations on Fees

THIS APPENDIX DERIVES a simple (partial equilibrium) system for calculating the impact of a cutback in government subsidies on private payments. It is assumed that the total amount of financial resources (R) to finance a certain consumption flow of social services is the sum of government subsidy allocations from general revenues (S) and private payments (H):

(C-1) $$R = S + H.$$

These revenues are spent on expenditures (E) that are equal to the unit cost (c) of providing the social services times the amount of social service (q) which is measured by the flow of homogeneous units (such as student years in the case of education) at a given quality level, z: $E = cq$. Unit costs are, in general, a function of q and z. The exact nature of this relationship depends upon the existence of scale economies. For costs to equal revenue,

(C-2) $$R = E = qc(q, z).$$

Government contributions, S, are assumed to be a control variable, the level of which is determined outside the system. Household payments are assumed to be equal to fee payments:

(C-3) $$H = pq^d$$

where p is the fee needed to buy a unit of social service of a given quality. The demand for the qualitatively homogeneous social service, q^d, is a function of household income (y), fee payments, and the quality (z) of the service that is provided. The latter variable is meant to capture some of the nonfee costs, such as transport, that need to be incurred in consumption:

(C-4) $$q^d = q^d(p,y,z).$$

To simplify the system, assume that the impact of quality on unit cost is zero and then substitute equations (C-2) and (C-3) into (C-1) to form

(C-5) $$q\,c(q) = S + pq^d.$$

At equilibrium, supply equals demand, so that

(C-6) $$q = q^d$$

and equations (C-4), (C-5), and (C-6) can be solved for three unknowns: q, q^d, and p.

Equilibrium to Equilibrium

One interesting issue is to determine the impact of change in S on the amount of fee changes needed to maintain a certain level of quality, under the assumption that the system is in equilibrium before and after the subsidy change. In figure B-1 this is equivalent to estimating the change from p_0 to p_1 if the subsidy provided by the government were to fall from S_0 to S_1. Equilibrium requires that the system move from points G to H.

To measure responsiveness, equations C-4 and C-6 are substituted into equation C-5 and the modified equation is then completely differentiated to form the system

(C-7) $$J\,dp = dS - [c - p + q(\partial c/\partial q)]\,(\partial q/\partial y)\,dy \\ - [c - p + q\,(\partial c/\partial q)]\,(\partial c/\partial z)\,dz$$

where $J = [q(\partial c/\partial q) + c - p](\partial q/\partial p) - q = [(ec + s)\,\eta - p](q/p)$; $s = c - p =$ the unit subsidy provided by the government; $\eta \equiv (p/q)(\partial q/\partial p) \equiv$ the fee elasticity of demand for the social service; and $e \equiv (q/c)(\partial c/\partial q) \equiv$ the elasticity of unit cost with respect to output.[1] As special cases, two assumptions are made about e, and these are discussed below. The results are summarized in table C-1.

---

1. The relationship between total cost elasticity e_C and average cost elasticity e is straightforward. By definition, $c(q) = C(q)/q$. Thus, $\partial c/\partial q = q[\partial C/\partial q - C]/q^2$. This implies that $e = (q/c)(\partial c/\partial q) = (q/C)\,(\partial C/\partial q) - 1 = e_C - 1$. Most cost function studies estimate e_C.

Table C-1. The Impact of a Change in Government Transfers on Fees, Costs, and Household Payments under Equilibrium

	The impact of a change in S on percentage change in		
Assumptions	Fees ($\dot{p}$)	Revenues ($\dot{R}$)	Household payments ($\dot{H}$)
Variable costs ($e, e_C \neq 0$)			
$\dot{z} = \dot{y} = 0$	$\dot{S} / \{[(ec/s) + 1]\eta - \phi\}$	$\eta \dot{p}$	$\dot{p} + \dot{R}$
$z = z(p), \dot{y} \neq 0$	$(\dot{S} - \varepsilon \dot{y}) / \{[(ec/s) + 1](\eta + \gamma\theta) - \phi\}$	$(\eta + \gamma\theta)\dot{p}$	$\dot{p} + \dot{R}$
Constant unit costs ($e = 0$)			
$\dot{z} = \dot{y} = 0$	$[1/(\eta - \phi)] \dot{S}$	$\eta \dot{p}$	$\dot{p} + \dot{R}$
$z = z(p), \dot{y} \neq 0$	$[1/(\eta + \gamma\theta - \phi)] [\dot{S} - \varepsilon \dot{y}]$	$(\eta + \gamma\theta)\dot{p}$	$\dot{p} + \dot{R}$

Note:
- p = unit fees
- c = unit cost
- C = total cost
- R = total revenue
- H = household payments
- S = government payments
- $\dot{x}$ = percentage change in x
- q = units of the service provided
- z = quality of q
- y = household income
- $s = c - p$
- $\phi = p/s$
- $\eta = (p/q)(\partial q / \partial p)$ = fee elasticity of demand
- $\gamma = (z/q)(\partial q / \partial z)$ = quality elasticity of demand
- $\theta = (p/z)(\partial z / \partial p)$ = fee elasticity of quality
- $e = (q/c)(\partial c / \partial q)$ = unit cost elasticity
- $\varepsilon = (y/q)(\partial q / \partial y)$ = income elasticity of demand

The first case assumes that there are no scale economies. Thus, long-run average costs are constant. If c were constant, then $\partial c/\partial q = 0$ implies that $e = 0$. With c, y, z held fixed, equation C-7 can be solved for the impact on fees of a cutback in S:

$$dp = \{p/[(s\eta - p)q]\} dS.$$

With the appropriate substitutions and after the multiplication of both sides of the equation by (S/p), the changes can be written in percentage change terms as

(C-8) $$\dot{p} = [1/(\eta - \phi)]\dot{S}$$

where the dot ($\cdot$) signifies percentage changes and $\phi \equiv p/s \equiv$ the price-to-unit subsidy ratio, which is assumed to be stable. For $\eta = -0.15$ and a fee-to-subsidy ratio of $\phi = 0.1$, a 10 percent cut in government expenditures would be financed by a fee increase of $[1/(-0.15 - 0.1)](-10) = 40$ percent.

The change in total revenue caused by the percent change is, from differentiation of equation C-2, under the assumption that c is fixed:

(C-9) $$\dot{R} = \eta \dot{p}.$$

With the above numbers, a fee increase of 40 percent will cause a change in the total cost of providing the social service of $(-0.15)(40) = -0.6$ percent.

The impact on household payments will be, from differentiation of equation C-3,

(C-10) $$\dot{H} = (\dot{p} + \dot{R}) = (1 + \eta)\dot{p}.$$

With the above numbers, household fee payments will change by $(40 - 6) = 34$ percent.

The preceding formulas hold under the assumption that, when government revenues are cut, other parameters that affect the demand, such as y and z, do not change. These conditions, of course, do not need to hold. In particular, Birdsall (1983a) argues that quality is affected by fees. The exact specification of this relationship $z = z(p)$ cannot be determined without assumptions about government behavior. But if z were endogenous in the system (equation C-5), it can be shown that the determinant is $\Delta = s(\partial q/\partial p) + s(\partial q/\partial z)(\partial z/\partial p) - q = (s\eta + s\gamma\theta - p)(q/p)$, where $\gamma \equiv (\partial q/\partial z)(z/q) \equiv$ quality elasticity of demand and $\theta \equiv (\partial z/\partial p)(p/z) \equiv$ the percentage increase in quality as a result of a percentage increase in fee payments. Assume for the moment that $\theta = 1$. Then,

$$dp = \{p/[s(\eta + \gamma) - p]q\} \, dS.$$

After appropriate substitutions,

(C-11) $$\dot{p} = [\dot{S}/(\eta + \gamma - \phi)].$$

If income were to change, for reasons completely external to the system, simultaneously with the change in the availability of government funds,

(C-12) $$\dot{p} = (\dot{S} - \varepsilon\dot{y})/(\eta + \gamma - \phi)$$

where $\varepsilon \equiv (\partial q/\partial y)(y/q) \equiv$ the income elasticity of demand.

The second case assumes variable costs. Schools and health services may face U-shaped long-run average cost curves because of scale economies and diseconomies. These services may operate on the downward sloping portion of these curves. If so $(\partial c/\partial q) < 0$. The amount of fee increase needed to finance a drop in government transfers of $\dot{S}$ is, in percentage terms,

(C-13) $$\dot{p} = \dot{S}/\{[(ec/s) + 1]\eta - \phi\}.$$

This implies the change in revenue, $\dot{R} = \eta\dot{p}$. Thus, household payments are

(C-14) $$\dot{H} = \dot{p} + \dot{R}.$$

Household Expenditures

The effect of a change in p on the share of a social service in total household expenditures can be calculated by differentiating $H_T = (H + H_0)/y$ where H = fee payments and H_0 = other expenditures on the social service. This yields $\dot{H}_T = [H/(H + H_0)]\dot{H} - \dot{y}$ if $\dot{H}_0 = 0$. The coefficient of $\dot{H}$ is the share of fee payments in total household expenditures on the social service.

Impact of a Fee Increase under a Fixed Subsidy Allocation with Excess Demand

The general formula for a subsidy constraint is

(C-15) $$[c(q) - p]q = s.$$

This simply states that the difference between total provider-borne cost $[qc(q)]$ and revenues received from user charges (pq) must be made by a subsidy allocation (S). To determine the impact of a marginal fee (p) increase on the quantity provided (q), with S held fixed, the equation is totally differentiated:

(C-16) $$[c(q) - p]dq + q[c'dq - dp] = 0.$$

The resulting equation is then rearranged as follows:

(C-17) $$(c - p + qc')dq = qdp.$$

Then, this can be solved for the following expression:

(C-18) $$\begin{aligned} dq/dp &= q/[c(e + 1) - p] \\ \dot{q} &= \dot{p}/[(c/p)(e + 1) - 1] \end{aligned}$$

when $e = c'(q/c)$ = unit cost elasticity of quantity expansion. If $e = 0$, the expression is equal to $p/(c - p)$, or the ratio of the fee to unit subsidy, times the change in price.

D

Tables

Table D-1. Cost-Recovery Ratios in Education, 1980

Country	Government (user fees as percentage of unit public cost) Primary	Secondary	Higher	Social[a] (private cost as percentage of total social cost) Primary	Secondary	Higher
East Africa						
Botswana	0.0	2.7	0.0	0.0	17.6	0.0
Burundi	0.0	6.3	14.8	0.0	18.8	21.6
Kenya	4.0	43.7	0.0	18.0	31.2	0.0
Lesotho	9.0	42.1	5.0	19.7	30.7	18.3
Malawi	37.0	38.0	1.0	29.0	29.3	17.0
Swaziland	7.0	26.3	—	19.0	25.4	—
Uganda	27.0	24.3	—	25.7	24.8	—
Zambia	3.0	11.6	—	17.7	20.5	—
Zimbabwe	0.0	5.0	—	0.0	18.3	—
West Africa						
Burkina Faso	13.0	0.0	0.0	21.0	0	0.0
Central African Rep.	2.5	2.7	—	17.5	17.6	—
Guinea	0.0	0.0	0.0	0.0	0.0	0.0
Mauritania	0.0	0.0	0.0	0.0	0.0	0.0
Nigeria	30.0	39.0	12.4	26.7	29.7	20.8
Sierra Leone	1.5	20.3	—	17.2	23.4	—
Togo	13.0	5.0	—	21.0	18.3	—
Asia						
India	2.0	18.5	29.1	17.3	22.8	26.4
Indonesia	0.0	9.0	13.0	0	19.7	21.0
Korea	3.7	41.2	23.4	17.9	30.4	24.5

(Table continues on the following page.)

Table D-1 (continued)

	Government (user fees as percentage of unit public cost)			Social[a] (private cost as percentage of total social cost)		
Country	Primary	Secondary	Higher	Primary	Secondary	Higher
Malaysia	5.0	5.0	5.8	18.3	18.3	18.6
Pakistan	1.2	1.8	2.1	17.1	17.3	17.4
Philippines	—	—	3.7	—	—	17.9
Solomon Islands	0.0	25.0	0.0	0.0	25.0	0.0
Thailand	0.0	12.5	6.9	0.0	20.8	19.0
Turkey	0.0	0.0	15.0	0.0	—	21.7
Latin America						
Bolivia	0.8	0.4	1.0	16.9	16.8	17.0
Brazil	—	—	5.0	—	—	18.3
Chile	1.6	0.9	25.0	17.2	17.0	25.0
Colombia	—	—	3.4	—	—	17.8
Costa Rica	0.3	0.5	8.0	16.8	16.8	19.3
Dominican Republic	0.0	0.0	1.0	0.0	0.0	17.0
Ecuador	0.0	0.0	2.0	0.0	0.0	17.3
Guatemala	—	—	10.0	—	—	20.0
Haiti	6.8	3.4	—	18.9	17.8	—
Honduras	0.0	9.6	10.0	0.0	19.9	20.0
Paraguay	4.1	2.0	0.7	18.0	17.3	16.9
Uruguay	0.5	0.4	5.0	16.8	16.8	18.3

— Not available.

a. Calculated from government columns using equation 2-6 in text.

Sources: Calculated from Wolff (1984) for East Africa; Ainsworth (1984), World Bank data, Tilak and Varghese (1985), Benson and Harbison (1985) for West Africa; Schiefelbein (1985) for Asia and Latin America, except Gomez (1984) for Colombia and Ainsworth (1984) for Bolivia and Haiti.

Table D-2. The Components of Public Educational Recurrent Expenditure
(percent)

Country	Year	Salaries	Materials	Scholarship	Other
Bolivia	1979	87.4	—	0.3	12.3
Botswana	1979	57.6	*	14.2	28.3
Burkina Faso	1979	51.5	10.3	37.7	0.5
Burundi	1979	63.0	0.4	17.5	4.7
Central African Rep.	1978	73.0	4.8	17.5	4.7
Guinea	1979	62.8	*	*	37.2
Haiti	1979	88.7	*	0.6	10.7
Indonesia	—	—	—	—	—
Kenya	—	—	—	—	—
Korea, Rep. of	1977	92.9	4.4	0.4	3.0
Lesotho	—	—	—	—	—
Malawi	1979	72.2	4.1	—	23.6
Mauritania	—	—	—	—	—
Mauritius	1979	73.8	0.2	*	26.0
Sierra Leone	—	—	—	—	—
Swaziland	1977	73.7	—	—	27.3
Tanzania	1979	35.2	15.9	13.2	35.7
Togo	1979	57.8	5.0	10.6	26.6
Uganda	1975	60.8	26.0	4.8	8.5

— Not available.
* Incorporated in salaries.
Source: Unesco, *1982 Statistical Yearbook,* table 4.2.

Table D-3. Social Returns to Higher Education by Subject
(percent)

Country	Agriculture	Engineering	Sciences	Medicine	Social sciences	Humanities	Economics	Arts	Law
Developing countries									
Brazil	5.2	17.3	—	11.9	—	—	16.1	—	17.4
India	—	16.6	—	—	—	12.7	—	—	—
Iran	13.8	18.2	14.2	—	—	15.3	18.5	—	—
Malaysia	9.8	13.4	—	12.4	—	—	—	—	15.0
Philippines	3.0	10.3	—	—	—	—	10.5	—	15.0
Developed countries									
Belgium	—	—	8.0	11.5	—	—	9.5	—	6.0
Canada	—	2.0	—	—	—	—	9.0	—	—
Denmark	—	8.0	—	5.0	—	—	9.0	—	10.0
France	—	—	12.3	—	—	—	16.5	—	16.5
Norway	2.2	8.7	6.2	3.1	—	—	8.9	4.3	10.6
Sweden	—	7.5	—	13.0	—	—	9.0	—	9.5
United Kingdom	—	11.4	11.0	—	13.0	—	—	13.5	—
Developing countries average	8.0	15.2	14.2	12.2	n.a.	14.0	15.0	—	16.2
Developed countries average	2.2	7.5	9.4	8.2	13.0	n.a.	10.3	8.9	10.5

— Not available.
Source: Psacharopoulos (1982), table 9. Reprinted with permission.

Table D-4. Share of Educational Subsidies by Income Group
(percent)

Country	Survey year	Type of subsidy	Income group		
			Poorest 30%	*Middle 30%*	*Upper 40%*
Chile	1983	Preprimary	50	35	15
		Primary	53	29	18
		Secondary	37	35	28
		University	15	24	61
		All levels	39	29	32
			Poorest 40%	*Middle 40%*	*Upper 20%*
Colombia	1979	Primary	59	36	6
		Secondary	39	46	16
		University	6	35	60
		All levels	40	39	21
			Poorest 40%	*Middle 30%*	*Upper 30%*
Indonesia	1978	Primary	51	27	22
		Junior secondary	45	21	33
		Senior secondary	22	23	55
		University	7	10	83
		All levels	46	25	29
Malaysia	1974	Primary	50	40	9
		Secondary	38	43	18
		Postsecondary	10	38	51
		All levels	41	41	18

Note: All rows total 100 percent except for rounding.

Sources: Castañeda (1984) for Chile; Selowsky (1979) for Colombia; Meesook (1984) for Indonesia; and Meerman (1979) for Malaysia.

Table D-5. The Structure of the Health Sector in Developing Countries: Types of Services and Providers

	Central government					Regional, provincial, and district government agencies	Local government and community organizations		Industrial and agricultural enterprises, parastatal and private	Private voluntary organizations, missions, and other	Private practitioners, modern and traditional
Health services	Health ministry	Social security agency	Other agencies[a]	Public works and other support agencies			Municipalities	Villages			
Personal care of patients											
Health facilities (hospitals, centers, physicians' offices)											
Outpatient											
General	*	*	*	—		*	*	—	*	*	*
Maternal and child health	*	*	*	—		*	*	—	*	*	**
Family planning	*	*	**	—		**	**	—	**	**	**
Inpatient											
General (bed and nursing)	*	*	*	—		*	*	—	*	*	*
Special services (deliveries, surgery, nutrition rehabilitation)	*	*	*	—		*	*	—	*	*	*
Village health care											
Preventive	*	—	—	—		*	—	*	—	*	*
Curative	**	—	—	—		**	—	**	—	**	**

152

Disease control programs
Vector control (spraying for malaria mosquitos)
Population prophylaxis (mobile teams immunize or deparasitize whole villages)
Environmental intervention (removing vegetation from stagnant waterways to control schistosomiasis)

Drug sales[b]

Other programs
Sanitation
Human waste disposal
General sewerage
Inspection (of food purveyors and processors)
Education and promotion of health and hygiene
Institutions (schools)
Media (radio, posters)

Table D-5 (continued)

Health services	Central government					Regional, provincial, and district government agencies	Local government and community organizations		Industrial and agricultural enterprises, parastatal and private	Private voluntary organizations, missions, and other	Private practitioners, modern and traditional
	Health ministry	Social security agency	Other agencies[a]	Public works and other support agencies			Municipalities	Villages			
Control of pests and zoonotic diseases											
Domesticated animals	*	—	—	*	*	—	—	*	—	—
Wild animals	*	—	—	*	*	—	—	—	—	—
Control of pollution											
Air	*	—	—	*	*	—	—	—	—	—
Water (from industrial sources)	*	—	—	*	*	—	—	—	—	—
Monitoring of communicable diseases	*	—	—	*	*	*	*	—	—	—

* Service is offered by providers in this category.
— Service not offered.

Note: Examples in parentheses are merely illustrative and not a complete list of possibilities.

a. For example, defense ministries that provide health services for military personnel; also police agencies, prisons, and mental institutions that provide services for their employees and inmates.

b. Drug sales to individuals by private or public pharmacies, excluding drugs sold or provided free as part of services under "Personal care of patients" above.

Source: de Ferranti (1985), table 1.

References

Ainsworth, Martha. 1983. "The Demand for Health and Schooling in Mali: Results of the Community and Service Provider Survey." World Bank, Country Policy Department, Discussion Paper 1983-7. Washington, D.C., March.

———. 1984. "User Charges for Cost Recovery in the Social Sectors: Current Practices." World Bank, Country Policy Department, Discussion Paper 1984-6. Washington, D.C., March.

Ainsworth, Martha, François Orivel, and Punam Chuhan. 1983. "Cost Recovery for Health and Water Projects in Rural Mali: Household Ability to Pay and Organizational Capacity of Villages." In *Three Studies on Cost Recovery in Social Sector Projects.* World Bank, Country Policy Department, Discussion Paper 1983-8. Washington, D.C., July.

Akin, John, Charles Griffin, David Guilkey, and Barry Popkin. 1982. "The Demand for Primary Health Care in the Bicol Region of the Philippines." Paper presented at the National Council for International Health Conference, Washington, D.C., June 14-16.

Anderson, D. L. 1980. "A Statistical Cost Function Study of Public General Hospitals in Kenya." *Journal of Developing Areas* 14:223-35.

Armitage, Jane, and Richard Sabot. Forthcoming. "Efficiency and Equity Implications of Subsidies of Secondary Education in Kenya." In David Newbery and Nicholas Stern, eds., *The Theory of Taxation for Developing Countries.* New York: Oxford University Press.

Behrman, Jere, and Nancy Birdsall. 1983. "The Quality of Schooling: Quantity Alone is Misleading." *American Economic Review* 73:926-96.

Benson, Charles, and Ralph Harbison. 1985. *"Nigeria—Education Investment Review."* World Bank, Education and Training Department. Washington, D.C. Preliminary draft.

Berry, R. A. 1980. "Education, Income Productivity and Urban Poverty." In Timothy King, ed., *Education and Income.* World Bank Staff Working Paper 402. Washington, D.C.

Bertrand, Trent, and Robert Griffin. 1983. "The Economics of Financing Education: A Case Study of Kenya." World Bank, Country Policy Department, Discussion Paper. Washington, D.C., December.

Besley, T. J., D. L. Bevan, and Paul Collier. 1985. "Health Insurance and Cost Recovery in

Developing Countries." World Bank, Population, Health, and Nutrition Department. Washington, D.C., October.

Bird, R. M. 1976. *Charging for Public Services: A New Look at an Old Idea.* Canadian Tax Papers 59. Toronto: Canadian Tax Foundation, December.

Birdsall, Nancy. 1980. "The Cost of Siblings: Child Schooling in Urban Colombia." *Research in Population Economics* 2:115–50.

———. 1983a. "Demand for Primary Schooling in Rural Mali: Should User Fees Be Increased?" In *Three Studies on Cost Recovery in Social Sector Projects.* World Bank, Country Policy Department, Discussion Paper 1983–8. Washington, D.C., July.

———. 1983b. "Strategies for Analyzing Effects of User Charges in the Social Sectors." World Bank, Country Policy Department, Discussion Paper 1983–9. Washington, D.C., September.

———. 1985. "Cost Recovery in Health and Education: Bank Policy and Operations." World Bank, Population, Health, and Nutrition Department. Washington, D.C. Processed.

Birdsall, Nancy, and Punam Chuhan. 1983. "Willingness to Pay for Health and Water in Rural Mali: Do WTP Questions Work?" In *Three Studies on Cost Recovery in Social Sector Projects.* World Bank, Country Policy Department, Discussion Paper 1983–8. Washington, D.C., July.

Blomqvist, A. G. 1979. *The Health Care Business: International Evidence on Private versus Public Health Care Systems.* Vancouver: Fraser Institute.

———. 1982. "Education, Unemployment and Government Job Creation for Graduates in LDCs." In T. E. Barker, A. S. Downes, and J. A. Sackey, eds., *Perspectives on Economic Development: Essays in Honour of W. Arthur Lewis.* Washington, D.C.: University Press of America.

Briones, G. 1983. "La Distribución de la Educación in el Modelo de Economia Neo-Liberal: 1974–1982." Santiago, Chile: Programa Interdisciplinario de Investigaciones en Educación (PIIE), Academia de Humanismo Cristiano. July.

Brodersohn, Mario S., and Maria Ester Sanjuro. 1978. "Seminario sobre Financiamiento de la Educación en América Latina." In Mario S. Brodersohn and Maria Ester Sanjuro, eds., *Financiamiento de la Educación en América Latina.* Mexico City: Fondo de Cultura Economica and Banco Interamericano de Desarrollo (Inter-American Development Bank).

Cameron, John, and Paul Hurst. 1983. *International Handbook of Education Systems: Sub-Saharan Africa, North Africa, and the Middle East,* vol. 2. New York: Wiley.

Carnoy, Martin, Henry Levin, Reginald Nugent, Suleman Sumra, Carlos Torres, and Jeff Unsicker. 1982. "The Political Economy of Financing Education in Developing Countries." In *Financing Educational Development,* conference proceedings, IDRC-205e. Ottawa: International Development Research Centre. May.

Castañeda, Tarsicio. 1984. "La Evolución del Gasto Social en Chile y su Impacto Redistributivo." University of Chile, Department of Economics. December. Processed.

Cochrane, Susan H. 1979. *Fertility and Education: What Do We Really Know?* Baltimore, Md.: Johns Hopkins University Press.

Cochrane, Susan H., Donald J. O'Hara, and Joanne Leslie. 1980. *The Effects of Education on Health.* World Bank Staff Working Paper 405. Washington, D.C.

Cowen, Robert, and Martin McLean. 1984. *International Handbook of Education Systems: Asia, Australasia, and Latin America*, vol. 3. New York: Wiley.

Culyer, A. J. 1980. *The Political Economy of Social Policy*. Oxford, Eng.: Martin Robertson.

de Ferranti, David. 1983. "Health Sector Financing and Expenditure in Developing Countries: Current Issues." World Bank, Population, Health, and Nutrition Department. Washington, D.C., February 8. Draft.

———. 1985. *Paying for Health Services in Developing Countries: An Overview*. World Bank Staff Working Paper 721. Washington, D.C.

de Tray, Dennis. 1984. "Schooling in Malaysia: Historical Trends and Recent Enrollments." Rand Note N-2011-AID. Santa Monica, Calif.: Rand Corp. October.

de Wulf, Luc. 1975. "Fiscal Incidence Studies in Developing Countries." *IMF Staff Papers* 22:61–131.

Donaldson, D. S. n.d. "An Analysis of Health Post-Based Insurance Schemes in the Lalit per District, Nepal." USAID Paper. Washington, D.C.: U.S. Agency for International Development. Processed.

Dougherty, Christopher, and George Psacharopoulos. 1977. "Measuring the Cost of Misallocation of Investment in Education." *Journal of Human Resources* 12(4):446–59.

Dunlop, David W. 1982. "Health Care Financing: Recent Experience in Africa." Paper prepared for the Conference on Health and Development in Africa, University of Bayreuth, Germany, June.

Eicher, J. C. 1984. "L'Enseignement Supérieur en Afrique de l'Ouest Francophone: Synthèse de Cinq Etudes de Cas." World Bank, Education and Training Department. Washington, D.C., August.

———. 1985. *Educational Costing and Financing in Developing Countries with Special Reference to Sub-Saharan Africa*. World Bank Staff Working Paper 655. Washington, D.C.

Feldstein, Martin, M. A. Piot, and T. K. Sunderesan. 1973. "Resource Allocation Model for Public Health Planning: A Case of Tuberculosis Control." In *Bulletin of the World Health Organization*, vol. 48, supplement.

Fields, Gary S. 1974. "Private Returns and Social Equity in the Financing of Higher Education." In David Court and D. P. Ghai, eds., *Education, Society and Development: New Perspectives from Kenya*. Nairobi: Oxford University Press.

———. 1980. "Education and Income Distribution in Developing Countries." In Timothy King, ed., *Education and Income*. World Bank Staff Working Paper 402. Washington, D.C.

Foxley, Alejandro, Eduardo Animat, and J. P. Arellano. 1979. Redistributive Effects of Government Programs. Oxford, Eng.: Pergamon.

Friedman, Milton. 1971. "Government Revenue from Inflation." *Journal of Political Economy* (July/August).

Gillis, Malcolm, and C. E. McClure. 1978. "Taxation and Income Distribution: The Colombian Tax Reforms of 1974." *Journal of Development Economics* 5:233–48.

Gomez, H. 1984. *Finanzas Universitarias*. Bogotá: Fedesarollo.

Hanovice, Karen. 1984. "The Private Higher Education Sector in Indonesia: Description and

Loan Feasibility." World Bank, East Asia and Pacific Projects Department. Washington, D.C. Processed.

Hauptman, A. M. 1983. "Student Loan Default Rates in Perspective." American Council on Education. Washington, D.C., February.

Haveman, Robert, and Barbara Wolfe. 1984. "Schooling and Economic Well-Being: The Role of Nonmarket Effects." *Journal of Human Resources* 19:377–407.

Heller, Peter S. 1975. *Issues in the Costing of Public Sector Outputs: The Public Medical Services of Malaysia.* World Bank Staff Working Paper 207. Washington, D.C.

———. 1979. "The Underfinancing of Recurrent Development Costs." *Finance & Development* 16(1):38–41.

———. 1981. "Testing the Impact of Value-Added and Global Income Tax Reforms in Korean Tax Incidence in 1976. *IMF Staff Papers* 28:375–410.

———. 1982. "A Model of the Demand for Medical and Health Services in Peninsular Malaysia." *Social Science and Medicine* 16:267–84.

Heller, Peter, and Joan Aghevli. 1985. "The Recurrent Cost Problem: An International Overview." In John Howell, ed., *Recurrent Costs and Agricultural Development.* London: Overseas Development Institute.

Heller, Peter, and Adrienne Cheasty. 1984. "Sectoral Adjustment in Government Expenditure in the 1970s: The Education Sector in Latin America." *World Development* 12(10): 1039–49. Published by Pergamon Journals Ltd., Oxford, U.K.

Herrick, Allison B., Howard R. Shavlach, and Linda Seville. 1974. *Intercountry Evaluation of Education Credit Institutions in Latin America.* Washington, D.C.: U.S. Agency for International Development.

Heyneman, Stephen P. 1975. "Changes in Efficiency and in Equity Accruing from Government Involvement in Ugandan Primary Education." *African Studies Review* 18(1):51–60.

Heyneman, Stephen P., Dean T. Jamison, and Xavier Montenegro. 1984. "Textbooks in the Philippines: Evaluation of the Pedagogical Impact of a Nationwide Investment." *Education Evaluation and Policy Analysis* 6(2):139–50.

Heyneman, Stephen P., and William A. Loxley. 1983. "The Effect of Primary-School Quality on Achievement across Twenty-Nine High- and Low-Income Countries." *American Journal of Sociology* 88(6):1162–94.

Hicks, Norman, and Anne Kubisch. 1984. "Cutting Government Expenditures in LDCs." *Finance & Development* 21(3):37–39.

Hinchliffe, Keith. 1985. *Issues Related to Higher Education in Sub-Saharan Africa.* World Bank Staff Working Paper 780. Washington, D.C.

Horton, Susan, and Pierre Claquin. 1983. "Cost Effectiveness and User Characteristics of Clinic-Based Services for Diarrhea." *Social Science and Medicine* 17:721–9.

International Monetary Fund. 1981. 1982. *Government Financial Statistics.* Washington, D.C.

Jallade, Jean-Pierre. 1973. *The Financing of Education: An Examination of Basic Issues.* World Bank Staff Working Paper 157. Washington, D.C.

Jamison, Dean T., and Lawrence J. Lau. 1982. *Farmer Education and Farm Efficiency.* Baltimore, Md.: Johns Hopkins University Press.

Jimenez, Emmanuel. 1985. "Selecting the Brightest: The Impact of a Hypothetical Policy Reform in Colombia." World Bank, Education and Training Department. Washington, D.C.

———. 1986a. "The Structure of Educational Costs: Multiproduct Cost Functions for Primary and Secondary Schools in Latin America." *Economics of Education Review* 5(1):25–40.

———. 1986b. "The Public Subsidization of Education and Health in Developing Countries: A Review of Equity and Efficiency." *World Bank Research Observer* 1(1):111–29.

Jimenez, Emmanuel, and Jee-Peng Tan. 1985. "Educational Development in Pakistan: The Role of User Charges and Private Schools." World Bank, Education and Training Department, Discussion Paper 16. Washington, D.C., December.

King, E. M., and L. A. Lillard. 1983. "Determinants of Schooling Attainment and Enrollment Rates in the Philippines." Rand Note N-1962-AID. Santa Monica, Calif.: Rand Corp. April.

Kolobe, Paki, and Tsie Pekeche. 1980. *A Survey of the Financial Status of the Private Health Association of Lesotho's Hospitals.* Maseru: Ministry of Health and Social Welfare, October. Processed.

Kondrassis, A. J., and S. C. Tseng. 1976. "The Demand for Higher Education in Taiwan: A Case Study." *International Journal of Social Economics* 3(3):146–66.

Krashinsky, Michael. 1981. *User Charges in the Social Services: An Economic Theory of Need and Ability.* Ontario Economic Council Research Study 22. Toronto: University of Toronto Press.

Krueger, A. O. 1974. "The Political Economy of Rent-Seeking Society." *American Economic Review* 64(3):291–303.

Kulakow, A. M., J. Brace, and J. Morrill. 1978. "Mobilizing Rural Community Resources for Support and Development of Local Learning Systems in Developing Countries." Washington D.C.: Academy for Educational Development.

Lee, K. H. 1984. "Universal Primary Education: An African Dilemma." World Bank, Education and Training Department. Washington, D.C.

———. 1985. "Further Evidence on Economies of Scale in Higher Education." World Bank, Education and Training Department. Washington, D.C. Processed.

Lee, K. H., and Jee-Peng Tan. 1984. "The International Flow of Third Level LDC Students to DCs: Determinants and Implications." *Higher Education* 13:687–90.

Lesotho, Government of. 1983. *Cost and Financing of Education in Lesotho.* Maseru: Ministry of Education. February.

Lim, David. 1983a. "Government Recurrent Expenditure and Economic Growth in Less Developed Countries." *World Development* 11(4):377–80.

———. 1983b. "Instability of Government Revenue and Expenditure in Less Developed Countries." *World Development* 11(5):447–50.

Lluch, Constantino, Alan A. Powell, and Ross A. Williams. 1977. *Patterns in Household Demand and Saving.* New York: Oxford University Press.

Lucas, R. E. B. 1984. "Selectivity in Use of Educational and Health Facilities in Sind." World Bank, Country Policy Department. Washington, D.C., March.

Mahar, Dennis J., and William R. Dillinger. 1983. *Financing State and Local Government in Brazil: Recent Trends and Issues.* World Bank Staff Working Paper 612. Washington, D.C.

Malawi, Government of. 1984. *The Impact of the Increase in School Fees on Primary School Enrollments in 1983.* Lilongwe: Ministry of Education and Culture. June.

Mann, A. J. 1982. "The Mexican Tax Burden by Family Income Class." *Public Finance Quarterly* 10(3):305-31.

Mbanefoh, G. F. 1980. "Sharing the Costs and Benefits of University Education in Nigeria." *International Journal of Educational Development* 1(2):231-43.

Meerman, Jacob. 1979. *Public Expenditure in Malaysia: Who Benefits and Why.* New York: Oxford University Press.

———. 1980. *Implementing Programs of Human Development.* World Bank Staff Working Paper 403. Washington, D.C.

———. 1982. "Cost Recovery in a Project Context: Some World Bank Experience in Tropical Africa." World Bank, Western Africa Regional Office. Washington, D.C., November.

Meesook, Oey A. 1984. *Financing and Equity in the Social Sectors in Indonesia: Some Policy Options.* World Bank Staff Working Paper 703. Washington, D.C.

Meier, G. M. 1976. *Leading Issues in Economic Development.* New York: Oxford University Press.

Mills, Michael. 1984. "Some Reflections on the Financing of the Health Sector in Zimbabwe." Paper presented at Conference on Financing in the Social Sector, World Bank, Washington, D.C., April.

Mingat, Alain, and George Psacharopoulos. 1985. "Financing Education in Sub-Saharan Africa." *Finance & Development* 22(1):35-38.

Mingat, Alain, and Jee-Peng Tan. 1985a. "On Equity in Education Again: An International Comparison." *Journal of Human Resources* 20(Spring):298-308.

———. 1985b. "Subsidization of Higher Education versus Expansion of Primary Enrollments: What Can A Shift of Resources Achieve in Sub-Saharan Africa?" *International Journal of Educational Development* 5(4):259-68.

———. 1986a. "Who Profits from the Public Funding of Education? A Comparison of World Regions." *Comparative Education Review* 30(2):260-70.

———. 1986b. "On the Quality of Education in Developing Countries: Another View." Paper presented at a conference on the Economics of Education: Tackling the New Policy Issues. Dijon: Institut de Recherche sur l'Economie de l'Education (IREDU).

———. 1986c. "Expanding Education through User Charges: What Can Be Achieved in Malawi and Other LDCs?" *Economics of Education Review* 5(8):273-86.

Mingat, Alain, Jee-Peng Tan, and Monzurul Hoque. 1984. "Recovery of Cost of Public Higher

Education in LDCs: To What Extent Are Loan Schemes an Efficient Instrument?" World Bank, Education and Training Department. Washington, D.C.

Muñoz, I. C., and Hernandez, M. A. 1978. "Financiamiento de la Educación Privada en América Latina." In Mario S. Brodersohn and Maria Ester Sanjuro, eds., *Financiamiento de la Educación en América Latina.* Mexico: Fondo de la Cultura Economica and Banco Interamericano de Desarrollo.

Musgrove, Philip. 1983. "Family Health Care Spending in Latin America." *Journal of Health Economics* 2(3):245–58.

Orivel, François. 1983. "Costs and Financing of Education in Upper Volta." World Bank, Country Policy Department, Discussion Paper 1984–5. Washington, D.C., August.

Pakistan, Government of. 1983. *The Sixth Five Year Plan, 1983–88.* Quetta.

Perraton, Hillary, Dean T. Jamison, Janet Jenkins, François Orivel, and Laurence Wolff. 1983. *Basic Education and Agricultural Extension: Costs, Effects, and Alternatives.* World Bank Staff Working Paper 564. Washington, D.C.

Piñera, Sebastian, and Marcelo Selowsky. 1981. "The Optimal Ability: Education Mix and the Misallocation of Resources within Education." *Journal of Development Economics* 8:111–31.

Prescott, Nicholas, and Dean T. Jamison. 1984. "Health Sector Finance and Expenditures in China." *World Health Statistics Quarterly* 37:387–402.

Prescott, Nicholas, and Jeremy Warford. 1982. "Economic Appraisal in the Health Sector in LDCs." World Bank, Population, Health, and Nutrition Department. Washington, D.C., February 10. Draft.

Psacharopoulos, George. 1977. "The Perverse Effects on Public Subsidization of Education or How Equitable is Free Education?" *Comparative Education Review* 21(2):69–90.

———. 1982. "The Economics of Higher Education in Developing Countries." *Comparative Education Review* 25(2):139–59.

———. 1984. "The Contribution of Education to Economic Growth: International Comparisons." In John Kendrick, ed., *International Comparisons of Productivity and Causes of the Slowdown.* Cambridge, Mass.: Ballinger.

———. 1985. "Returns to Education: A Further International Update and Implications." *Journal of Human Resources* 20(4):584–604.

Psacharopoulos, George, and William Loxley. 1985. *Diversified Secondary Education and Development.* Baltimore, Md.: John Hopkins University Press.

Psacharopoulos, George, and Maureen Woodhall. 1985. *Education for Development: An Analysis of Investment Choices.* New York: Oxford University Press.

Ram, Rati. 1982. "Public Subsidization of Schooling and Inequality of Educational Access: A New World Cross Section Study." *Comparative Education Review* 26(1):36–47.

Richards, Peter J. 1982. "Meeting Basic Health Care Needs." In P. J. Richards and M. A. Leonor, eds., *Target Setting for Basic Needs: The Operation of Selected Government Services.* Geneva: International Labour Office.

Rogers, Daniel C. 1972. "Student Loan Programs and the Returns to Investment in Higher

Levels of Education in Kenya." *Economic Development and Cultural Change* 20(2):243–59.

Roth, Gabriel. 1987. *Private Provision of Public Services in Developing Countries.* New York: Oxford University Press.

Saunders, Robert J., and Jeremy Warford. 1976. *Village Water Supply: Economics and Policy in the Developing World.* Baltimore, Md.: John Hopkins University Press.

Schiefelbein, Ernesto. 1985. "Education Costs and Financing Policies in Latin America." World Bank, Education and Training Department. Washington, D.C.

Selowsky, Marcelo. 1979. *Who Benefits from Government Expenditure?* New York: Oxford University Press.

Selowsky, Marcelo, and Lance Taylor. 1973. "The Economics of Malnourished Children." *Economic Development and Cultural Change* 22(1):17–30.

Somerset, H. C. A. 1974. "Who Goes to Secondary School? Relevance, Reliability and Equity in Secondary School Selection." In David Court and D. P. Ghai, eds., *Education, Society and Development.* Nairobi: Oxford University Press.

Squire, Lyn. 1981. *Employment Policy in Developing Countries.* New York: Oxford University Press.

Stinson, Wayne, and American Public Health Association. 1982. "Community Financing of Primary Health Care." In *Primary Health Care Issues,* ser. 1, no. 4. Washington, D.C.: American Public Health Association.

Swaziland, Government of. 1981. *The Status and Development of Education in the Kingdom of Swaziland.* Mbabane: Ministry of Education. November.

Tan, Jee-Peng. 1985a. "Private Direct Cost of Secondary Schooling in Tanzania." *International Journal of Educational Development* 5(1):1–10.

———. 1985b. "Private Enrollments and Expenditure on Education: Some Macro Trends." *International Review of Education* 31(1):103–17.

Tan, Jee-Peng, K. H. Lee, and Alain Mingat. 1984. *User Charges for Education: The Ability and Willingness to Pay in Malawi.* World Bank Staff Working Paper 661. Washington, D. C.

Tanzania, Government of. 1984. *Educational System in Tanzania Towards the Year 2000.* Dar es Salaam: Ministry of Education, October.

Thobani, Mateen. 1983. *Efficiency and Equity Implications of User Charges in Social Sector Services: The Financing of Education in Malawi.* World Bank Staff Working Paper 572. Washington, D.C.

Thorndike, R. L. 1973. *Reading Comprehension in Fifteen Countries.* New York: Wiley

Tilak, Jandhyala, and N. V. Varghese. 1985. *Discriminatory Pricing in Education.* Occasional Paper 8. New Delhi: National Institute of Educational Planning and Administration.

Unesco. *Statistical Yearbook.* Paris, various years.

———. 1981. *World School-Age Population until the Year 2000: Some Implications for the Education Sector.* Paris.

———. 1982. *Development of Education in Africa: A Statistical Review.* Paris.

———. 1985. *Education Statistics—Latest Year Available.* Paris, January.

USAID (U.S. Agency for International Development). 1982. *Recurrent Costs Problems in Less Developed Countries.* USAID Policy Paper. Washington, D. C., May.

Vu, My T. 1984. *World Population Projections 1984: Short- and Long-Term Estimates by Age and Sex with Related Demographic Statistics.* Washington, D. C.: World Bank.

Watson, Keith. 1981. "The Higher Education Dilemma in Developing Countries: Thailand's Two Decades of Reform." *Higher Education* 10:297–314.

WHO (World Health Organization). 1981. "Review of Health Expenditures, Financial Needs of the Strategy for Health for All by the Year 2000, and the International Flow of Resources for the Strategy." Report by the Director-General to the Executive Board. Document WHO/EB69/7. November.

Williams, Peter. 1974. "Lending for Learning: An Experiment in Ghana." *Minerva* 12(July):326–45.

Wolff, Laurence. 1984. *Controlling the Costs of Education in Eastern Africa: A Review of Data, Issues, and Policies.* World Bank Staff Working Paper 702. Washington, D.C.

Woodhall, Maureen. 1983. *Student Loans as a Means of Financing Higher Education: Lessons from International Experience.* World Bank Staff Working Paper 599. Washington, D.C.

World Bank. 1980a. *Education.* Sector Policy Paper. Washington, D.C.

———. 1980b. *Health.* Sector Policy Paper. Washington, D.C.

———. 1980c. *World Development Report 1980.* New York: Oxford University Press.

———. 1983. *World Development Report 1983.* New York: Oxford University Press.

———. 1984a. *World Development Report 1984.* New York: Oxford University Press.

———. 1984b. *Toward Sustained Development in Sub-Saharan Africa: A Joint Program of Action.* Washington, D.C.

———. 1986. *Financing Education in Developing Countries: An Exploration of Policy Options.* Washington, D.C.

Zschock, Dieter. 1986. "Medical Care under Social Insurance in Latin America: Review and Analysis." *Latin American Research Review* 21(1):99–122.

Index

Ability of students, 31, 49, 51, 72, 95, 97
Ability to pay, 22–23, 72, 79, 97
Access to services, 1, 2, 49–51. *See also* Queue for services; Rationing
Accountability, 3, 39, 45, 95, 104
Achievement in school, 23, 61, 72, 73, 100, 104
Administrative costs: of distributing subsidies, 72, 104; of student loans, 100; of taxes, 32, 125; of user fees, 2, 7, 90, 106, 124–25
Admission to school. *See* Student selection
Africa: education in, 13–15, 21–22, 51, 102, 126, 127; health services in, 15, 33, 42, 114–15, 127; public expenditures for education in, 3, 15, 21, 40, 41, 42, 52–54, 84–85, 90, 95, 97–98; public expenditures for health services in, 33, 114–15; user fees for education in, 6, 14–15, 20, 79, 87–88, 97–98, 102, 127; user fees for health services in, 127
Ainsworth, Martha, 22
Akin, John, 110
Allocation: of resources, 2, 3, 27, 35, 39, 43, 45, 53, 57, 66, 139–40; of services, 11, 22–23, 49–51, 106, 108; of user fee revenue, 5–6, 14–15, 35, 82, 87, 114–16, 124
Alma-Ata declaration (World Health Organization), 31

Asia: education in, 6, 12–13, 21, 51, 72, 79n1, 102, 105; health services in, 20, 23, 57, 110, 112, 116–17, 121, 127; public expenditures in, 15, 20, 21, 23, 57, 59, 101, 105; user fees for education in, 15, 87, 96–98; user fees for health services in, 116–17, 121, 127

Bangladesh, 113
Basic human needs, 26, 133–34
Behrman, Jere, 90–91
Benefit-cost ratio, 31, 59, 124
Benefits, 3, 23, 25, 74, 125, 140; of education, 5, 27n, 28, 50–51, 100, 103, 104; of health services, 41–42, 106, 108, 119. *See also* Externalities; Private marginal benefit; Social marginal benefit
Birdsall, Nancy, 90–91, 127, 145
Bolivia, 21, 83, 87, 88
Botswana, 23, 127
Brazil: education in, 29, 90–91, 99, 105; health services in, 42
Budget, 5, 15, 27, 32–33, 45, 66; for education, 6, 14, 21, 40, 41, 84–85, 93; for health services, 42, 114. *See also* Public expenditures
Budget constraints, 1, 3, 26, 33, 45, 48, 65, 67, 73, 76, 139; for education, 49, 77, 83, 84, 87–88, 92, 93, 102; for health services, 118

Budget deficits, 1, 2, 93
Budget surplus, 140
Burkina Faso, 53, 90
Burundi, 127

Cameroon, 22, 102, 127
Capital costs, 13, 67n1, 126, 136, 137, 138
Capital market. *See* Financial markets
Capital stock, 27, 28, 45, 47, 48, 137
Caribbean, 15, 99
Carnoy, Martin, 28–29
Central government, 14, 27, 35–42, 45, 49, 124, 139
Cheasty, Adrienne, 95
Chile: public expenditures in, 21, 101; user fees in, 22, 87, 102
China, 59, 126, 127
Citizenship, education and, 28, 41
Claquin, Pierre, 113
Colombia: education in, 21, 22, 51, 59, 95, 96, 99, 101, 102; health services in, 57, 112, 121, 123; public expenditures in, 21, 57, 59, 101; user fees in, 22, 102, 105, 112, 121, 123
Comoros, 95
Competition for government resources, 1, 33, 74
Congo, People's Republic of the, 22, 102
Consumption, 23n, 25, 35, 41, 48, 50, 57, 131, 136. *See also* Optimal consumption; Underconsumption
Consumption costs, 11, 20, 58, 59, 74
Cooperative schools. *See* Harambee schools
Costs. *See* Administrative costs; Capital costs; Consumption costs; Education costs; Health care costs; Nonfee costs; Opportunity costs; Private costs; Private marginal cost; Recurrent costs; Social costs; Social marginal cost; Transport costs; Unit costs
Cost recovery, 1–2, 4–5, 26, 35, 133, 138, 140–41; definition of, 11–12; in education, 5–6, 12–20, 22, 77–78, 82–87, 88, 102–03; in health services, 6–7, 20–21, 116, 118; of private providers, 12, 21–22; social, 12, 15, 17, 20–21
Costa Rica, 99
Côte d'Ivoire, 53, 84–85
Credit, 5, 6, 25, 95, 98–100, 127. *See also* Student loans
Curative health services, 6, 39, 41, 42, 51, 62, 106, 108–11, 114, 118. *See also* Hospital care; Outpatient care
Curriculum development, 21, 22, 102

de Ferranti, David, 41
Demand, 5, 35, 42–43, 59, 66, 69–71, 73, 74–76, 143, 145; for education, 5, 40, 50, 77–79, 84, 87–91, 103, 137; for health services, 6–7, 51, 106, 108–11, 114–18. *See also* Excess demand; Social demands; Supply
Disease control, 25, 29, 31, 41, 106, 107
Dominican Republic, 87
Donaldson, D. S., 121
Drug sales, 20, 41, 48, 59, 106, 115, 127

Earnings. *See* Income; Wages
East Africa, 95
East Asia, 6
Economic rents, 74, 100
Economies of scale, 2, 5, 26, 65, 144; in education, 78, 82–83, 87; in health services, 112–13, 115, 118, 121; in schools, 136–38
Education. *See* Free education; Higher education; Primary education; Rural education; Secondary education; Urban education
Education costs, 13–14, 17, 58–59, 60–61, 78–83, 84, 87, 104. *See also* Unit costs
Education fees, 5, 22, 48, 79, 87, 92, 95, 101–05, 125. *See also* Cost recovery; Higher education, pricing of; Primary education, pricing of; Secondary education, pricing of
Education subsidies, 6, 14, 25, 52–54, 77, 82, 90, 91–92, 97, 104–05, 126. *See also* Higher education, public

Education subsidies (*continued*)
  expenditures for; Primary education, public expenditures for; Secondary education, public expenditures for
Efficiency, 1–4, 23–26, 65–74, 124, 125, 131; in education, 22, 40–41, 50–51, 60, 82, 83, 88, 91, 92–100, 104; in health services, 7, 23, 41–42, 51, 106, 108, 115, 118–21; social, 82
Egypt, 29
El Salvador, 17
Enrollment, 21, 49, 73, 78, 82–83, 97; in primary schools, 3, 12, 79, 85, 90, 92; in secondary schools, 12–13, 66, 79, 87, 88, 126; in universities, 3–4, 13, 23, 61, 84, 87, 90, 95
Entrance examinations, 23, 51, 60–62, 72, 87, 100
Equilibrium, 5, 76, 92, 116, 139, 140. *See also* Partial equilibrium analysis
Equity, 1–2, 4, 26, 52, 57–62, 71–74, 125; in education, 6, 22, 52–54, 97, 98, 101–02, 103; in health services, 7, 23, 54–57, 106, 121–23
Ethiopia, 22, 95, 102
Excess demand, 3, 22, 23, 58, 68, 114–15, 139, 140, 141, 146
Externalities, 2, 5, 23, 25–26, 39, 49, 65, 67–71, 72, 74, 133; in education, 40–41, 43, 77, 90, 103; in health services, 6, 41–42, 43, 106, 107–08
Extracurricular materials, 4, 51

Farmers, 28, 54
Financial markets, 59, 72, 73–74, 98–100
Fixed costs. *See* Capital costs
Free education, 2, 3, 13, 50
Free primary education, 15, 22, 48, 90, 102
Free health services, 3, 4, 23, 118

Gambia, 127
Ghana, 127
Government. *See* Central government

Government expenditures. *See* Public expenditures
Government guarantee: of student loans, 73–74, 98; of health insurance, 73
Grade repetition, 51, 61, 100
Graduates, 51, 66, 95; wages of, 25–26, 40, 135
Greece, 84

Harambee schools (Kenya), 21, 87, 100, 126
Health care costs, 21, 59, 108, 118, 123. *See also* Hospital care; Unit costs
Health care subsidies, 6–7, 21, 25, 42, 51, 54–57, 106–08, 116, 121–23
Health fees, 6–7, 15, 20, 21, 22–23, 41–42, 51, 108, 114–16, 119–23, 127
Health insurance, 5, 7, 21, 25, 51, 73, 106, 118–21, 123, 127
Health services. *See* Curative health services; Hospital care; Preventive health services; Primary health care; Public health services; Rural health services; Urban health services
Heller, Peter S., 45, 95
Higher education, 25, 39, 41, 43, 51, 65, 124; pricing of, 1, 5–6, 17, 22, 68, 71–72, 77, 83–87, 101–02; public expenditures for, 3, 4, 14, 40, 41, 49, 52–53, 84, 101, 127
Higher-income households, 57–58, 59, 60–62; and education, 4, 51, 53–54, 101; and health care, 51, 121–23
Honduras, 99
Horton, Susan, 113
Hospital care, 5, 41, 42, 72, 73, 106, 108; costs of, 43, 112–13, 115, 118, 127; subsidies for, 4, 15, 57, 138
Hospital size, 112–13
Household choices, 1, 50, 57, 78, 104, 108
Human capital, 25, 31, 59, 67

Illness, 29, 31, 42, 108, 115, 119, 121
Immunization, 23, 41, 65, 107

Income, 31, 57, 58, 69, 141, 145; and education, 2, 3, 17, 27n, 49, 54, 78, 95–97; forgone, 2, 3, 17, 25; and health care, 20, 54–57, 106, 108, 116–17, 121–23; redistribution of, 16, 97
Income groups. *See* Socioeconomic groups
Income tax, 4, 57, 72, 125
Indirect taxes, 1, 57, 125
Indonesia: education in, 15, 22, 59, 84, 96, 101; health services in, 57, 127
Inpatient care. *See* Hospital care
Inputs, 25, 43–49, 93–95
International Monetary Fund, 32
Investment, 26n, 45, 59; in education, 2, 3, 27–29, 40, 51, 79, 103, 125; in health care, 29, 31, 42, 73. *See also* Public expenditures; Underinvestment
Iran, 57
Ivory Coast. *See* Côte d'Ivoire

Jamaica, 95, 99
Jimenez, Emmanuel, 88
Jordan, 22, 102

Kenya: education in, 15, 21, 22, 48, 87, 90, 100, 126; health services in, 113
Korea, Republic of, 29, 87

Labor market, 25–26, 29, 40
Labor productivity, 29, 31, 41
Labor unions, 49, 93
Latin America: education in, 6, 12–13, 17, 83, 84, 98–99, 100; health services in, 112, 119–21; public expenditures for education in, 20, 21, 29, 33, 41, 59, 90–91, 95, 101; public expenditures for health services in, 15, 33, 42, 46–47, 57; user fees for education in, 22, 87, 88, 102, 105; user fees for health services in, 123
Lesotho, 14–15, 21, 127
Lim, David, 47–48
Literacy, 23, 28, 41

Living allowances, 3, 6, 13–14, 40, 73, 84, 88, 127
Loans. *See* Student loans
Local financing of services, 14, 104–05, 125, 126
Lower-income households, 25, 57, 58–59; and education, 2–3, 6, 17, 50, 51, 57, 72, 97, 101–02, 104, 105; and health care, 22–23, 51, 57, 97, 123

Malawi: education in, 15, 22, 79, 84–85, 87–88, 97–98, 100; health services in, 114
Malaysia: education in, 58–59, 96–97, 101; health services in, 15, 57, 110, 112, 116–17, 121, 123
Mali: education in, 53, 90, 91; health services in, 114
Marginal benefit. *See* Private marginal benefit; Social marginal benefit
Marginal cost. *See* Private marginal cost; Social marginal cost
Marginal cost pricing, 23, 25, 26, 68, 76, 83, 102, 113n, 131, 146
Mauritius, 21, 51
Medical insurance. *See* Health insurance
Merit goods, social services as, 25, 65. *See also* Public goods
Mexico, 21, 99
Middle East: education in, 22, 29, 102; health services in, 15, 59
Mingat, Alain, 54
Moral hazard, health care and, 119
Morbidity, 108, 113
Morocco, 127

Needs assessment: distribution of subsidies and, 57, 72, 104; health care and, 4, 118, 140
Nepal, 121
Nigeria, 22, 84, 102
Nonfee costs, 58–59, 102, 126, 143

Opportunity costs, 15, 20, 21, 27n, 62, 74; of education, 17, 43, 50, 58, 78; of health services, 42

Optimal consumption, 38, 66–68, 133–34, 135, 140
Optimal pricing, 136, 138, 139
Outpatient care, 4, 41, 43, 51, 65, 108, 110, 112, 127

Pakistan: education in, 72, 87, 102, 105; health services in, 127
Paraguay, 83, 88
Partial equilibrium analysis, 5, 131, 142–46
Peru, 21
Philippines: education in, 21; health services in, 23, 57, 110, 127
Physicians, 4, 42, 73, 119
Piñera, Sebastian, 51
Population growth, 2, 28, 31, 35
Preventive health services, 39, 41, 107–08. *See also* Disease control; Immunization
Price discrimination, 22, 72, 73, 74
Prices: definition of, 1, 11; low, 3, 4, 23, 39, 65, 71–73, 139, 140. *See also* User fees
Pricing policy, 22–26, 65–67, 69–74, 124–27. *See also* Marginal cost pricing; Uniform pricing; User fees; Zero pricing
Primary education, 38, 39, 41, 65, 124; costs of, 27, 42–43, 59, 77–78, 83; pricing of, 2, 6, 15, 22, 48, 71, 73, 88–92; public expenditures for, 6, 21, 29, 52, 68, 84–85, 90, 91–92, 95, 101
Primary health care, 2, 31, 38, 59; pricing of, 42–43, 59, 73
Private costs, 2, 4, 11, 15, 22, 25, 42–43, 57–59, 69, 70–71, 73, 74–76, 139; of education, 3, 12, 27*n*, 50, 53; of health services, 20, 42
Private marginal benefit, 131, 133, 134, 135
Private marginal cost, 125, 131, 134
Private rate of return, 40, 59, 73, 79, 103. *See also* Social rate of return
Private schools, 14, 21, 22, 87, 102–05
Productivity: health and, 108; of labor, 29, 31, 41; schooling and, 49, 51

Public expenditures, 31–35, 67, 142, 144; for education, 13–15, 28–29, 93–95, 101; for health services, 15, 29, 31, 42, 46–47; for higher education, 3, 4, 14, 40, 41, 49, 52–53, 84, 101, 127; for primary education, 6, 21, 29, 52, 68, 84–85, 90, 91–92, 95, 101; for school-age children, 53–54, 57, 59; for secondary education, 14, 21, 41, 52, 53, 59, 95. *See also* Africa; Asia; Latin America; Local financing of services
Public goods, 65, 66, 68, 71, 77, 106, 136
Public health services, 4, 51, 121, 126; pricing of, 115–16; subsidies for, 57, 59, 114–15

Quality: of education, 85, 90–91, 102, 104, 137; of health care, 110, 112, 114–15; of social services, 1, 39, 48, 51, 142–43
Queue for services, 4, 51, 62, 115, 118

Rationing, 22, 58, 60, 74, 140; of education, 3–4, 23, 50–51, 60–62, 73, 100; of health services, 62, 115, 118
Recurrent costs, 43, 45–49, 67, 91, 95, 123, 126, 136–38, 145
Referral health services, 106, 127
Resource mobilization, 22, 66, 74, 84, 118, 125–26
Resources: allocation of, 2, 3, 27, 35, 39, 43, 45, 53, 57, 66, 139–40; competition for government, 1, 33, 74; redistribution of, 4, 41. *See also* Rationing; Tax revenue; User fee revenue
Revenue. *See* Cost recovery; Tax revenue; User fee revenue
Risk, 1, 25, 73, 119, 121
Rural education, 17, 28, 59, 79, 90, 95, 104
Rural health services, 4, 42, 57, 106, 113, 121
Rural social services, 5, 22, 59, 73, 125
Rwanda, 95, 126, 127

Scale economies. *See* Economies of scale
Scholarships, 14, 43, 53, 72, 97–98, 101, 102, 104, 105
School-age children: in Malawi, 88; public expenditures for, 53–54, 57, 59; wages of, 17, 79; work activity of, 58–59
Schools. *See* Achievement in school; Enrollment; Private schools; Student loans; Student selection; Student-teacher ratio; Teachers; Textbooks
Secondary education, 39, 51, 85, 124; costs of, 2, 17, 83, 88, 100, 126; pricing and, 77, 87–88; public expenditures for, 14, 21, 41, 52, 53, 59, 95
Selowsky, Marcelo, 51
Senegal, 42, 53, 84–85
Social costs, 12, 38, 40, 51, 97, 100, 123, 139
Social demands, 27, 35, 38, 70, 74, 102
Social efficiency, 82
Social insurance, 119–21
Social loss, 43, 92, 139
Social marginal benefit, 26, 51, 66, 85, 131, 133, 135
Social marginal cost, 35, 38, 68n, 131, 133, 137, 138
Social objectives, 27–35, 38
Social rate of return, 3, 39, 45, 70, 71; in education, 6, 27–28, 40–41, 68, 84, 85, 90; in health services, 29
Socioeconomic groups, 54, 60–62, 73, 83n, 100, 121. *See also* Higher-income households; Lower-income households
Sri Lanka, 57
Student loans, 51, 73, 95, 97, 98–100, 101
Student selection, 22, 92, 95–100, 102–04, 137
Students, ability of, 31, 49, 51, 72, 95, 97. *See also* Achievement in school
Student-teacher ratio, 48, 90
Sub-Saharan Africa, 3, 6, 40
Subsidies, 2, 3, 5, 26, 39, 43, 45, 127, 134; allocation of, 38, 49, 52, 57–59, 66–74, 76, 139–41, 142–46. *See also* Education subsidies; Health care subsidies

Sudan, 84–85
Supply, 69, 73, 74, 139–41, 146; of education, 78, 84, 90–91, 102–03; of health services, 106, 111–13. *See also* Demand
Swaziland, 14n
Sweden, 100

Taiwan, 79n1
Tan, Jee-Peng, 54
Tanzania, 84–85, 95, 127
Taxes: administrative costs and, 32, 125; education and, 28; exemption from, 105; revenue from, 1, 11, 57, 67, 82, 93. *See also* Income tax
Teachers, 21, 22, 48, 49, 90, 92, 93, 102; salaries of, 14n, 25
Tertiary-level education. *See* Higher education
Textbooks, 12, 13, 14–15, 49, 53, 60, 90, 95
Thobani, Mateen, 70, 139
Togo, 23, 84–85, 127
Transfer of funds, 12, 14, 31, 69, 90, 92, 145
Transport costs, 2, 22, 42, 58, 143; to health facilities, 20, 59; to schools, 15, 53, 79
Tuition, 3, 13, 27n, 73, 88, 97, 102, 127
Tutoring, 4, 51, 60

Uganda, 22
Underconsumption, 74, 84, 131, 138, 139
Underinvestment, 3, 35–38, 39, 67, 73
Uniform pricing, 42–43, 73, 134
Unit costs, 3, 15, 23, 35, 66–67, 69, 138, 142; of education, 13, 14, 82–83, 84n, 87, 88, 126; of health services, 42, 111–12, 115–18
United States, 98–99, 100
Universal education, 38, 85, 91
Universities. *See* Enrollment; Higher education
Urban education, 17, 28, 59, 77, 79, 87, 90, 104

Urban health services, 4, 42, 121
Urban social services, 5, 22, 73, 138
User-fee revenue, 4, 67–68, 70, 84, 133; allocation of, 5–6, 14–15, 35, 82, 87, 114–16, 124
User fees, 1, 66, 74–76, 126–27, 138, 142–46; administrative costs of, 2, 7, 90, 106, 124–25; exemption from, 101, 105; regulation of, 11, 21–23, 67–68, 70, 101–03, 105. *See also* Education fees; Health fees; Pricing policy
Utilization: of education, 91, 96; of health services, 108, 114, 118, 121; of social services, 42–43, 48, 66–67, 68*n*, 74, 76

Variable costs. *See* Recurrent costs
Venezuela, 21

Wages, 42, 62, 98, 121; of graduates, 25–26, 40, 135; of school-age children, 17, 79
Water supply programs, 41–42, 106
Welfare economics, 4–5, 14, 71–72, 74, 107
Willingness to pay, 3, 39, 49, 50, 68, 72, 136, 139; for education, 51, 79, 95; for health care, 116
Workers: education subsidies and, 54; health of, 29, 31, 42, 121
World Bank, 1, 13, 31, 33, 35, 51, 127
World Development Report 1984, 35
World Health Organization (WHO), 31

Zambia, 22, 102
Zero pricing, 5, 42, 43, 49–50, 65, 69, 74, 134
Zimbabwe, 15, 23, 127

The most recent World Bank publications are described in the catalog *New Publications,* which is issued in the spring and fall of each year. The complete backlist of publications is shown in the annual *Index of Publications,* which contains an alphabetical title list and indexes of subjects, authors, and countries and regions; it is of value principally to libraries and institutional purchasers. The continuing research program is described in *The World Bank Research Program: Abstracts of Current Studies,* which is issued annually. The latest edition of each is available free of charge from Publications Sales Unit, The World Bank, 1818 H Street, N.W., Washington, D.C. 20433, U.S.A., or from Publications, The World Bank, 66, avenue d'Iéna, 75116 Paris, France.